On
Humanism

A lucid account of humanism which combines the virtues of fairly balanced discussion and a passionate polemic. It deserves to become humanism's unofficial manifesto – the only kind a free thinking movement can have.

Julian Baggini, author of *Atheism, A Very Short Introduction*

Praise for the series

'. . . allows a space for distinguished thinkers to write about their passions'
The Philosophers' Magazine

'. . . deserve high praise'
Boyd Tonkin, *The Independent* (UK)

'This is clearly an important series. I look forward to reading future volumes.'
Frank Kermode, author of *Shakespeare's Language*

'both rigorous and accessible'
Humanist News

'the series looks superb'
Quentin Skinner

'. . . an excellent and beautiful series'
Ben Rogers, author of *A.J. Ayer: A Life*

'Routledge's Thinking in Action series is the theory junkie's answer to the eminently pocketable Penguin 60s series.'
Mute Magazine (UK)

'Routledge's new series, *Thinking in Action*, brings philosophers to our aid . . .'
The Evening Standard (UK)

'. . . a welcome new series by Routledge'
Bulletin of Science, Technology and Society (Can)

RICHARD NORMAN

On
Humanism

Routledge
Taylor & Francis Group

LONDON AND NEW YORK

First published 2004
by Routledge
11 New Fetter Lane, London EC4P 4EE

Simultaneously published in the USA and Canada
by Routledge
29 West 35th Street, New York, NY 10001

Routledge is an imprint of the Taylor & Francis Group

Typeset in Joanna MT by
RefineCatch Limited, Bungay, Suffolk
Printed and bound in Great Britain by
TJ International Ltd, Padstow, Cornwall

British Library Cataloguing in Publication Data
A catalogue record for this book is available from the British Library

Library of Congress Cataloging in Publication Data
Norman, Richard (Richard J.)
    On humanism / Richard Norman. – 1st ed.
       p.   cm. – (Thinking in action)
    1. Secular humanism. I. Title. II. Series.
    BL2747.6.N67   2004
    2.11'.6 – dc22   2003026288

ISBN 0-415-30522-5 (hbk)
ISBN 0-415-30523-3 (pbk)

Acknowledgements

I should like to thank Tony Bruce for his advice at all stages in the writing of this book, and Julian Baggini, Marilyn Mason and Tony Skillen for their valuable comments on previous drafts of the text, from which I have greatly benefited, even if I have sometimes been too stubborn to follow their suggestions. For parts of Chapter 5 I also had the benefit of discussion with colleagues in the departments of Philosophy and Film at the University of Kent, and further helpful comments from Sarah Cardwell. I have also had good help and feedback from Mat, Anna, Rob and Cathy. I would like to think that the book may have something to say to their generation.

Extracts from *Waterland* are reprinted in Chapter 5, by permission of A.P. Watt Ltd on behalf of Graham Swift.

> What a piece of work is a man! How noble in reason! how
> infinite in faculty! in form, in moving, how express and
> admirable! in action how like an angel! in apprehension how
> like a god! the beauty of the world! the paragon of animals![1]

Is this a statement of something we could call 'humanism'? It
comes from Shakespeare's *Hamlet*, and it is often quoted as a
celebration of the qualities that make us human, perhaps also
with the suggestion that recognising these qualities can inspire
us to use them to the full. If we look further, however, we find
that things are not so simple. The context of Hamlet's words is
not a declaration of faith in human life, but an expression of
despair. Our quoted passage is preceded by these words:

> I have of late, – but wherefore I know not, – lost all my mirth,
> forgone all custom of exercises; and indeed it goes so heavily
> with my disposition that this goodly frame, the earth, seems to
> me a sterile promontory; this most excellent canopy, the air,
> look you, this brave o'erhanging firmament, this majestical
> roof fretted with golden fire, why, it appears no other thing to
> me but a foul and pestilent congregation of vapours.

What looked like an optimistic affirmation of human potentialities was after all, then, part of a classic expression of how
human life can come to seem meaningless. Having enumerated

the qualities which make a man 'the paragon of animals', Hamlet continues:

> And yet, to me, what is this quintessence of dust? man delights not me; no, nor woman neither, though, by your smiling, you seem to say so.

Already, then, we are presented with some challenging questions for humanism. Whatever we may say, in the abstract, about the powers of reason and action which human beings possess, is this enough to sustain us in the practical business of making sense of our lives? There is also a serious question lurking in the throwaway phrase 'no, nor woman neither'. In the play we can recognise an allusion to Hamlet's already troubled relationship with Ophelia. There is also, however, a deeper question about the ambiguity of 'man'. It can be used neutrally to refer to human beings in general. It can also be used more narrowly to mark the contrast between the genders 'man' and 'woman'. Hamlet's half-jesting remark can therefore also be seen as posing a genuine problem: is humanism a philosophy of exclusion? In setting up an ideal of 'man', is it giving a privileged status to one part of the human species, and relegating to an inferior status those human beings – women, or perhaps the members of non-European cultures – who are excluded by the favoured model?

Finally we should look again at the words 'What a piece of work is a man'. If a human being is 'a piece of work', this suggests a workman who fashioned us – presumably a divine creator. The words 'angel' and 'god' likewise imply that this celebration of the human is located within a system of religious belief. How necessary is this? Can we maintain this elevated view of the human species only by thinking of man as created by God 'in his own image'? Or might we, on the contrary, suggest that humanism comes into its own when belief in God is rejected, when man usurps the place of God and is no longer seen as subservient to a higher, supernatural authority?

We can pursue this question by turning to another influential piece of writing, by someone who has certainly been called a 'humanist'. This is the Italian Renaissance philosopher Giovanni Pico della Mirandola, writing a century before Shakespeare. In his oration 'On the Dignity of Man' of 1486, Pico claims to identify 'the reason why man is rightly said and thought to be a great marvel and the animal really worthy of wonder'. Man, he says, was the last of living things to be created by God, and was then addressed by his creator in these words:

> 'We have given to thee, Adam, no fixed seat, no form of thy very own, no gift peculiarly thine, that thou mayest feel as thine own, have as thine own, possess as thine own the seat, the form, the gifts which thou thyself shalt desire. A limited nature in other creatures is confined within the laws written down by Us. In conformity with thy free judgment, in whose hands I have placed thee, thou art confined by no bounds; and thou wilt fix limits of nature for thyself. I have placed thee at the center of the world, that from there thou mayest more conveniently look around and see whatsoever is in the world. Neither heavenly nor earthly, neither mortal nor immortal have We made thee. Thou, like a judge appointed for being honorable, art the molder and maker of thyself; thou mayest sculpt thyself into whatever shape thou dost prefer. Thou canst grow downward into the lower natures which are brutes. Thou canst again grow upward from thy soul's reason into the higher natures which are divine.'[2]

According to Pico, then, the elevated status of human beings consists not in the possession of some fixed nature but in the capacity for free choice. Pico then urges us to use this freedom in order to distance ourselves from our animal desires, and to aspire to the condition of the angels, by cultivating the intellect for the study of philosophy and theology and thereby drawing closer to God. The second half of his oration is a proposal for a public disputation of nine hundred philosophical and theological theses which Pico has drawn up, appealing to the authority of the Christian and Hebrew scriptures, of the ancient Greek philosophers, of the writings of Islamic thinkers and of Zoroastrianism (the ancient religion of Persia), and of works on magic and the occult. Not only, then, is Pico's celebration of the dignity of man firmly located in a religious context. It is associated by him with what many modern humanists would regard as a motley collection of beliefs and superstitions, some of them bizarre.

Contrast this with a very different version of humanism. Here is a passage from a lecture *Why I Am Not a Christian*, delivered by the philosopher Bertrand Russell to a meeting of the National Secular Society in 1927:

> Science can teach us, and I think our own hearts can teach us, no longer to look round for imaginary supports, no longer to invent allies in the sky, but rather to look to our own efforts here below to make this world a fit place to live in, instead of the sort of place that the Churches in all these centuries have made it. We want to stand upon our own feet and look fair and square at the world – its good facts, its bad facts, its beauties, and its ugliness; see the world as it is, and be not afraid of it. Conquer the world by intelligence, and not merely by being slavishly subdued by the terror that comes from it. The whole conception of God is a conception derived from the ancient

Oriental despotisms. It is a conception quite unworthy of free men. When you hear people in church debasing themselves and saying that they are miserable sinners, and all the rest of it, it seems contemptible and not worthy of self-respecting human beings.[3]

For Russell, as for Pico, the dignity of human beings resides in their capacity to use their intelligence and to act as free men, but there the similarities end. According to Russell the natural ally of humanism is not religion but science. Religion and science are seen to be in conflict with one another, and a belief in the powers of human beings to make a good world for themselves is contrasted with the craven tendency of human beings to abase themselves before a god.

To complete my preliminary survey of some contrasting versions of humanism I turn to another lecture delivered by a twentieth-century philosopher. This is the French philosopher Jean-Paul Sartre's lecture *Existentialism is a Humanism*, given in Paris in 1945. 'Existentialism' was the label – not of his own choosing – which had come to be applied to Sartre's own philosophy. In linking it with humanism, Sartre suggests that 'the word humanism has two very different meanings'. One of these, he says, is the view 'which upholds man . . . as the supreme value' (and it may remind us of Pico's talk of man as 'a great marvel and the animal really worthy of wonder'):

Humanism in this sense appears, for instance, in Cocteau's story *Round the World in 80 Hours*, in which one of the characters declares, because he is flying over mountains in an aeroplane, 'Man is magnificent!' This signifies that although I, personally, have not built aeroplanes I have the benefit of those particular inventions and that I personally, being a man, can consider myself responsible for, and honoured by, achievements that are peculiar to some men. It is to assume that we can ascribe value to man according to the most distinguished deeds of certain men. That kind of humanism is absurd, for only the dog or the horse would be in a position to pronounce a general judgment upon man and declare that he is magnificent, which they have never been such fools as to do – at least, not as far as I know.[4]

Sartre's second sense of 'humanism' can remind us of Pico in another way; it focuses on the idea that human beings have no fixed nature but can make of themselves what they choose through their exercise of freedom.

> This is humanism, because we remind man that there is no legislator but himself; that he himself, thus abandoned, must decide for himself.
>
> (pp. 55–6)

Like Russell, Sartre sees this version of humanism as presupposing atheism. It is 'nothing else but an attempt to draw the full conclusions from a consistently atheistic position' (p. 56). In speaking of man as 'abandoned', Sartre means 'that God does not exist, and that it is necessary to draw the consequences of his absence right to the end' (pp. 32–3):

> When we think of God as the creator, we are thinking of him, most of the time, as a supernal artisan. . . . God makes man according to a procedure and a conception, exactly as the artisan manufactures a paper-knife, following a definition and a formula. . . . Atheistic existentialism . . . declares that . . . there is no human nature, because there is no God to have a conception of it. . . . Man is nothing else but that which he makes of himself.
>
> (pp. 27–8)

Sartre and Russell, then, share a humanism which is a belief in the 'human' in opposition to a belief in a god. Sartre would, however, be more hesitant about Russell's faith in science. He argues (more particularly in other writings) that the appropriate way of understanding human actions is importantly different from a scientific understanding of causally determined events in the natural world. Accordingly, in the lecture, he links his emphasis on human freedom with a sharp contrast between human beings and natural objects:

> this theory alone is compatible with the dignity of man, it is the only one which does not make man into an object. All kinds of materialism lead one to treat every man including oneself as an object – that is, as a set of pre-determined reactions, in no way different from the patterns of qualities and phenomena which constitute a table, or a chair or a stone. Our aim is precisely to establish the human kingdom as a pattern of values in distinction from the material world.
> (pp. 44–5)

We have now accumulated a number of questions to be asked about any view of the world to which we might be inclined to apply the label 'humanism':

> Does humanism imply a belief in a god who created human beings with a special status, or does it belong with the rejection of belief in a god?
>
> Is humanism the natural ally of religion, or of science, or of both, or of neither?
>
> Does humanism involve the belief that there are certain qualities unique and special to human beings and not possessed by any other entities in the natural world?

Does a belief in the ideal of 'man' function to exclude groups of human beings who do not match this favoured model of what it is to be human?

Is humanism a view of the world which we can live by and with which we can make sense of our lives?

I do not think that we can give a definitive answer to any of these questions, because I do not think that there is any definitive set of beliefs called 'humanism'. There are many humanisms. Apart from the possible versions which we have already glanced at, there are, as we shall see, other uses of the word which I have not yet mentioned. In the next section of this chapter I shall attempt to introduce some order into the apparent chaos, by tracing briefly some of the stages in the history of the word. I shall then, in the subsequent section, identify the sense in which I shall be using the term, and the version of humanism which I shall aim to defend in the rest of the book.

'HUMANISM' AND ITS HISTORY

The Italian word 'umanista' was coined, probably in the late fifteenth or early sixteenth century, to denote a scholar or teacher of the *humanities* – the disciplines of grammar, rhetoric, poetry, history and moral philosophy.[5] These studies were referred to by the Latin label *studia humanitatis*, a phrase which probably goes back to the fourteenth century and which implies a contrast between the study of 'humanity' and the study of divinity, of natural philosophy, and of vocational disciplines such as law and medicine. The humanists of the fourteenth to the sixteenth centuries, in Italy and in other European countries, were in particular interested in the study of the classical literature of ancient Greece and Rome, finding in it an ideal of human life which they wished to revive. Pico della Mirandola was one of these humanists, and *On the Dignity of Man* was, as we have seen, an explicit statement of the programme of reconciling the literature and thought of the ancient world with Christian religious belief. With his celebration of the distinctive human capacity for free choice, however, Pico does put a new slant on traditional Christian views of human nature, and more generally the Italian humanists represent a new emphasis on the value of human achievements in this life rather than seeing it simply as preparation for the life to come.

The first use of the corresponding abstract noun 'humanism' is in German. The word 'Humanismus' was similarly used in an educational context, in early nineteenth-century Germany, to refer to the traditional classical education built around the humanities. The retrospective application of the German noun to the thought and culture of fifteenth-century Italy was influentially established by Jacob Burckhardt's famous book *Die Cultur der Renaissance in Italien*, published in 1860. He speaks of humanism not just as an educational curriculum but as a broader cultural phenomenon, and he hints at the potential conflict with the Christian church.

> But now, as competitor with the whole culture of the Middle Ages, which was essentially clerical and was fostered by the Church, there appeared a new civilization, founding itself on that which lay on the other side of the Middle Ages.[6]

The same conception of 'Renaissance humanism' was propagated in English by John Addington Symonds in his multi-volume work *The Renaissance in Italy*. Volume II, 'The Revival of Learning', published in 1877, contains the following passage:

As I cannot dispense with the word Humanism in this portion of my work, it may be well to fix the sense I shall attach to it. The essence of humanism consisted in a new and vital perception of the dignity of man as a rational being apart from theological determinations, and in the further perception that classical literature alone displayed human nature in the plenitude of intellectual and moral freedom. It was partly a reaction against ecclesiastical despotism, partly an attempt to find the point of unity for all that had been thought and done by man, within the mind restored to consciousness of its own sovereign faculty. Hence the single-hearted devotion to the literature of Greece and Rome that marks the whole Renaissance era. Hence the watchword of that age, the *Litterae Humaniores*. Hence the passion for antiquity, possessing thoughtful men, and substituting a new authority for the traditions of the Church. Hence the so-called Paganism of centuries bent upon absorbing and assimilating a spirit no less life-giving from their point of view than Christianity itself. Hence the persistent effort of philosophers to find the meeting-point of two divergent inspirations. Hence, too, the ultimate antagonism between the humanists, or professors of the new wisdom, and those uncompromising Christians who, like S. Paul, preferred to remain fools for Christ's sake.[7]

What is interesting here is Symonds's attempt to insert a wedge between the umanisti and the Christian church, to point up what he sees as the latent anti-ecclesiastical tenor of Renaissance humanism and the implicit conflict with Christianity itself.

In order to trace the process by which the term 'humanism' came to be linked more closely with the rejection of religious belief, I need first to refer to another historical movement which feeds more directly into modern secular humanism – that of the Enlightenment, and especially of those eighteenth-century French Enlightenment thinkers referred to as 'les lumières' or 'les philosophes'. Though there are important differences between them, they share an attitude of scepticism towards, or outright rejection of, religious belief. They appeal to reason and experience against tradition, in order to criticise prejudice and superstition, to reject ideas of the supernatural and with them the tyranny of religious authority and political authority, each of which they see as reinforcing the other. A classic Enlightenment text is Baron d'Holbach's *Système de la Nature* of 1770.[8] Holbach seeks to understand Man as a part of Nature, governed like everything else by the laws of nature. He believes that by properly understanding themselves as part of nature, human beings will learn how to pursue their own happiness effectively, will recognise that happiness is achieved by living in peace and harmony with others, and that this, not a set of theologically sanctioned laws and commands, is the true nature of morality.

Man is the work of Nature: he exists in Nature: he is submitted to her laws: he cannot deliver himself from them; nor can he step beyond them even in thought. In vain his mind would spring forward beyond the visible world, an imperious necessity always compels his return. For a being formed by Nature, and circumscribed by her laws, there exists nothing beyond the great whole of which he forms a part, of which he experiences the influence. The beings which he pictures to himself as above nature, or distinguished from her, are always chimeras formed after that which he has already seen, but of which it is impossible he should ever form any correct idea, either as to the place they occupy, or of their manner of acting. . . . Instead, therefore, of seeking outside the world he inhabits for beings who can procure him a happiness denied to him by Nature let man study this nature, let him learn her laws, contemplate her energies, observe the immutable rules by which she acts: let him apply these discoveries to his own felicity and submit in silence to her mandates, which nothing can alter.[9]

Holbach himself is a thoroughgoing atheist. Though there had been other previous thinkers, from classical antiquity onwards, who had similarly rejected any religious belief, the French Enlightenment thinkers represent the first intellectual movement in modern European history to articulate a systematic non-religious philosophy with practical implications.

The same intellectual tradition is continued in early twentieth-century Germany, for example, by Ludwig Feuerbach, whose criticism of religion in The Essence of Christianity interprets the Christian idea of God as the projection onto an imagined divine supernatural being of what are essential human qualities.[10] Feuerbach was one of a number of thinkers labelled 'Left Hegelians', writing in the wake of Hegel (whose own philosophy of religion is finely balanced between orthodoxy and projectionism). The Left Hegelian who was in due course to become the most famous and influential was Karl Marx. In his 'Economic and Philosophical Manuscripts' of 1844 (which remained unpublished for almost a century), Marx contrasts atheism as 'a denial of God' – an alien being set above nature and man – with positive humanism.[11] For humanism to be realised in practice, however, requires the political and economic success of communism. With the appropriation by society of the means of production which are privately owned in a capitalist economy, work can become, for all, the objective expression of essential human powers, and the social and natural world can become humanised.

> Communism as completed naturalism is humanism, and as completed humanism is naturalism. It is the genuine solution of the antagonism between man and nature and between man and man.[12]

Marx's is one of the earliest uses of the term 'humanism' to refer to the positive side of atheism.

What was in late eighteenth-century France and early nineteenth-century Germany an intellectual tendency became in nineteenth-century Britain and elsewhere a broad popular movement, taking root in society and embodied in formal institutions. Such organisations did not at first make use of the terms 'humanist' and 'humanism' to describe themselves. Their preferred terms were those such as 'freethinker', 'secularist' and 'rationalist'. The most important such institutions to emerge in Britain were the Ethical Societies. These began as a breakaway movement from the Unitarian church (so called because it rejected the doctrine of the Trinity and the belief in the divinity of Jesus). The Ethical Societies gradually abandoned all religious beliefs and devoted themselves to the propagation of ethical values without any religious foundations. They came together to form the Union of Ethical Societies, which in 1920 became the Ethical Union. In the twentieth century the terms 'humanist' and 'humanism' came increasingly to be appropriated by people working and writing in this tradition, and in 1967 the Ethical Union became the British Humanist Association. Perhaps the most influential advocate of the term 'humanism' was

H. J. Blackham, who became Secretary of the Ethical Union in 1945 and subsequently the first Director of the British Humanist Association.

This brief historical sketch has highlighted the contrast between the essentially religious character of Renaissance humanism and the adoption of the term 'humanism' by those who wish to use it as a label for a non-religious system of belief. It is usually insisted that the two uses of the word 'humanism' are quite distinct, and that modern secular humanism has nothing to do with Renaissance humanism or with the use of the word to refer to an education grounded in the humanities – what we might call in general 'cultural humanism'. It is true that they are different, but it is not just a coincidence that the same word is used in these two different contexts. On the one hand, as we have seen, talk of cultural 'humanism' is not just a technical term to refer to a branch of the educational curriculum; it encapsulates the idea that the humanities are worth studying because they foster valuable features of human life and celebrate valuable qualities of human beings. From the other side, modern atheists and secularists, in adopting the word 'humanism', have deliberately been drawing on the older connotations of the term in the cultural tradition – connotations having to do with the assertion of human dignity and the celebration of what is finest in human thought and creativity. Their appropriation of the term is intended as a reminder of what human beings can achieve, as the positive and optimistic side of a non-religious world-view.

Secular humanism is the version of humanism I shall state and defend in this book – humanism as an alternative to religious belief. In the past, religion has furnished people with a practical philosophy of life, and it still does so for the majority of the world's population, providing answers to questions such as 'Why are we here?' and 'What is the purpose of human life?' For many of us, who can find no good reason for believing in the existence of a god or gods, those answers are no longer available. As I shall argue, there are no supernatural or super-human beings to tell us how to live. Although, in the contemporary world as a whole, religious believers are still very much in the majority, their numbers in a society such as modern Britain have declined dramatically over the past hundred years. That is a huge change, and we still have to get to grips with its implications. Humanism, then, in the sense in which I shall understand it, is an attempt to think about how we should live without religion.

ATHEISM AND AGNOSTICISM

I shall say more in Chapter 2 about the reasons for rejecting religious belief, but at this stage where we are concerned with definitions, I should add a word about the meaning of some key terms. By 'religion' I mean a view of the world based on a belief in the existence of a god or gods or supernatural beings. The word is sometimes used more widely than that, and some would even say that humanism is a religion, but I am using the word 'religion' in that specific sense. I use the word '*theist*' to refer to someone who believes in the existence of a god or gods. In contrast, an *atheist* is someone who believes that there is no god. It would therefore be gratifyingly simple to be able to say that humanists, in the sense in which I am using the word, are atheists, but things are not that simple. Many humanists prefer to describe themselves as 'agnostics' rather than atheists. An *agnostic* is someone who says that they do not know whether there is a god. They may say this because they think that the arguments and the evidence for and against the existence of a god are finely balanced and make it impossible to arrive at a clear decision. They may be more deeply agnostic, saying not just that it is difficult to decide, but that it is impossible to know whether there is a god. They may say, perhaps, that the limitations of human understanding put such knowledge beyond our reach. Given the range of versions of agnosticism, it could in practice go either way. One could be, say, a Christian agnostic or a Muslim agnostic, and go along with the religious practices and way of life while harbouring doubts. A humanist agnostic would be someone who, seeing no basis for a firm belief about the existence or non-existence of any divine being, concludes that in practice one should live as though there is no god. For my own part I should describe myself as an atheist. I adopt that label rather than 'agnostic' not as an expression of dogmatic certainty, but because I think that the onus is on those who believe in a god to provide reasons for that belief. If they cannot come up with good reasons, then we should reject the belief. In the same way, I cannot prove conclusively that there are no fairies, or witches, but I am not aware of any good evidence that such beings exist, and in the absence of such evidence I do not describe myself as an 'agnostic' about fairies or witches; I simply say that I do not believe in them. I take the same view about gods.

The rejection of religious belief need not mean a hostility to religion in all its manifestations. Many humanists, I know, are implacably opposed to religion and they can give reasons for being so. They can point to the ways in which religion has blighted people's lives, imposing restrictions and inhibitions in the name of divine commands which thwart people's aspirations to happiness, filling them with guilt for innocent pleasures and fear of eternal damnation. They can point to a long list of terrible things done in the name of religion: the medieval Crusades; the self-styled 'civilising' mission of Christian imperialism and the wiping out of the indigenous cultures of the Americas, Africa and the Pacific in the name of the Christian god; in the modern world, the continuing conflict between religious groups in Northern Ireland, and in the south Asian subcontinent, and the destructive fanaticism of Christian and Muslim and Hindu fundamentalists. I am less inclined than some humanists to condemn religion wholesale on these grounds, partly because I recognise that one could produce an equally horrific litany of crimes committed in the name of secular ideologies. I shall say more about this in a moment, but for now the point is simply to suggest that there are deeper causes of human destructiveness than the explicit beliefs which people hold. I recognise also that religion has inspired not only some of the worst but also some of the best human achievements. It has inspired social and political movements to improve the lot of human beings, such as the abolition of the slave trade, the civil rights movement, campaigns for peace and against world poverty and famine. It has inspired many of the greatest cultural and artistic achievements – the religious art of the Renaissance, magnificent works of music such as Handel's *The Messiah* and Bach's B-minor Mass, the great medieval cathedrals and innumerable other gems of ecclesiastical architecture. To present religion and its works in a wholly negative light would in my view be hopelessly unbalanced. My objection to religious belief is not that it is universally harmful but, simply, that it is false. If that is so, however, then we had better look for some alternative set of beliefs to live by, and that is the project of secular humanism.

OPTIMISM AND PESSIMISM

Some might say that the project is doomed to failure. That might be the view of a pessimistic atheist. An atheist, in other words, need not be a humanist. He or she might maintain that, since there is no god, life is utterly bleak and meaningless and there is nothing left for us but despair. A more élitist version of such a position might be that the great mass of mankind, in contrast to the enlightened few, cannot live without religion. Human weakness, it might be maintained, is such that most people will neither find any purpose in life, nor be able to cope with life's trials and tribulations, nor do what morally they ought to do, unless they are motivated by a belief in divine guidance and support. Therefore, if people need these psychological props, we had better not knock them away.

Humanists do not draw that conclusion. Humanism as I understand it involves not just the rejection of religious belief but, at the very least, the positive affirmation that human beings can find from within themselves the resources to live a good life without religion. Atheists who have adopted the term 'humanism' have, I suggested, wanted to mark the continuity with earlier celebrations of human dignity and human worth. With Shakespeare they are prepared to say 'What a piece of work is a man!' (or rather '. . . is a human being!'), and though like Hamlet they recognise that life can sometimes seem stale and flat they consider that a belief in human qualities can, by and large, sustain us.

That optimism however carries with it a danger, the danger of lapsing into naivety. I shall be looking at various criticisms of humanism in due course, but this one I want to confront from the start, because it affects my definition of the humanism which I want to defend. The tendency to naive optimism is apparent in some of the Enlightenment philosophers. They assume that the dead weight of superstition persists only because it is imposed by the unholy alliance of the spiritual authority of the priesthood and the temporal authority of tyrants. Remove that superstition, they imply, give enlightened reason room to work, and it will lead to the triumph of happiness and virtue. Since the happiness of each individual is naturally in harmony with the happiness of others, all that is needed to enable people to lead virtuous lives is that their characters should be formed by a rational education. The obstacle to this, the source of corruption, lies not in human nature but in the vested interests of the political and ecclesiastical powers.

There is perhaps also a corresponding tendency to naive optimism in the tradition of cultural humanism – in the idea that an education in the arts and literature will have an ennobling effect, that it will inevitably be morally improving. Both kinds of optimism have, historically, been encouraged by the prevalent ideology of 'progress' in the nineteenth century, fostered by the growth of industry and economic prosperity and by the spread of self-styled 'civilisation' from Europe to other parts of the globe.

Some people would say that all such optimism has been shattered by the experience of the twentieth century and its catalogue of horrors and atrocities. It was the century which saw the slaughter in the trenches in the First World War, the rise of Nazism and Stalinism, the concentration camps and the Holocaust, the massive destructiveness of the Second World War, the deliberate bombing of cities culminating in the dropping of the atomic bombs on Hiroshima and Nagasaki and ushering in an era when the human race is capable of eliminating itself completely in a nuclear war. What room does this leave for faith in humanity? These horrors have been perpetrated in the name of secular ideologies such as nationalism, communism, fascism and democracy. Some would see them as evidence of what human beings are bound to do when the constraints of religion are removed. For some religious believers they are confirmation of the doctrine of 'original sin', the belief that since there is a corruption at the heart of human nature, the salvation of human beings can come only from a transcendental source.

Can any kind of humanism be sustained in the light of the historical record of the past century? I think that it can, but I think also that our definition of humanism has to be refined to purge it of the remnants of implausible optimism. One example of this modest and sceptical humanism comes to us from the very depths of the twentieth-century experience. I have in mind Primo Levi's classic account of that most inhuman of all atrocities, the Nazi concentration camps. Levi's book is the record of his experience as a prisoner in Auschwitz. The framework through which Levi seeks to understand that experience is a humanism without illusions, the provisional humanism encapsulated in the title of the book: If This Is a Man.

I call Levi's humanism provisional because he knows all too well that a person's humanity is something which they can lose. It was the object of the camp at Auschwitz precisely to dehumanise its inmates:

> Then for the first time we become aware that our language lacks words to express this offence, the demolition of a man. In a moment, with almost prophetic intuition, the reality was revealed to us: we had reached the bottom. It is not possible to sink lower than this; no human condition is more miserable than this, nor could it conceivably be so. Nothing belongs to us any more; they have taken away our clothes, our shoes,

even our hair; if we speak, they will not listen to us, and if they listen, they will not understand. They will even take away our name: and if we want to keep it, we will have to find ourselves the strength to do so, to manage somehow so that behind the name something of us, of us as we were, still remains. . . . Imagine . . . a man who is deprived of everything he loves . . . he will be a hollow man, reduced to suffering and needs, forgetful of dignity and restraint, for he who loses all often easily loses himself.[13]

The camp's aim of dehumanising its inmates was one which could all too easily be achieved, but, just for that reason, the aspiration to remain human could still function as a value, perhaps the only value to which it was possible to cling:

After only one week of prison, the instinct for cleanliness disappeared in me. I wander aimlessly around the washroom when I suddenly see Steinlauf, my friend aged almost fifty, with nude torso, scrub his neck and shoulders with little success (he has no soap) but with great energy. Steinlauf sees me and greets me, and without preamble asks me severely why I do not wash. Why should I wash? Would I be better off than I am? Would I please someone more? Would I live a day, an hour longer? . . .

But Steinlauf interrupts me. He has finished washing and is now drying himself with his cloth jacket which he was holding before wrapped up between his knees and which he will soon put on. And without interrupting the operation he administers me a complete lesson . . . that precisely because the Lager was a great machine to reduce us to beasts, we must not become beasts; that even in this place one can survive, and therefore one must want to survive, to tell the story, to bear witness; and that to survive we must force ourselves to save at least the skeleton, the scaffolding, the form of civilization. We are slaves, deprived of every right, exposed to every insult, condemned to certain death, but we still possess one power, and we must defend it with all our strength for it is the last – the power to refuse our consent. So we must certainly wash our faces without soap in dirty water and dry ourselves on our jackets. We must polish our shoes, not because the regulation states it, but for dignity and propriety. We must walk erect, without dragging our feet, not in homage to Prussian discipline but to remain alive, not to begin to die.[14]

The camp at Auschwitz dehumanised not only its victims but also its functionaries, who by destroying in themselves all traces of identification with their victims destroyed what was authentically human in themselves. In this inhuman hell the simplest actions stood out as a reminder of what it is to be human.

The story of my relationship with Lorenzo is both long and short, plain and enigmatic. . . . In concrete terms it amounts to little: an Italian civilian worker brought me a piece of bread and the remainder of his ration every day for six months; he gave me a vest of his, full of patches; he wrote a postcard on my behalf to Italy and brought me the reply. For all this he neither asked nor accepted any reward, because he was good and simple and did not think that one did good for a reward. . . .

I believe that it was really due to Lorenzo that I am alive today; and not so much for his material aid, as for his having constantly reminded me by his presence, by his natural and plain manner of being good, that there still existed a just world outside our own, something and someone still pure and whole, not corrupt, not savage, extraneous to hatred and terror; something difficult to define, a remote possibility of good, but for which it was worth surviving.

The personages in these pages are not men. Their humanity is buried, or they themselves have buried it, under an offence received or inflicted on someone else. The evil and insane SS men, the Kapos, the politicals, the criminals, the prominents, great and small, down to the indifferent slave Häftlinge, all the grades of the mad hierarchy created by the Germans paradoxically fraternized in a uniform internal desolation.

But Lorenzo was a man; his humanity was pure and uncontaminated, he was outside this world of negation. Thanks to Lorenzo, I managed not to forget that I myself was a man.[15]

I see Levi's book as one of the great documents of humanism, a humanism as hard-won as it could possibly be. His survival was, he says, in large part a matter of luck, but 'I was also helped by the determination, which I stubbornly preserved, to recognize always, even in the darkest days, in my companions and in myself, men, not things, and thus to avoid that total humiliation and demoralization which led so many to spiritual shipwreck.'[16]

Levi's book is testimony to a version of humanism which it is possible to defend without illusions. That is the humanism which I want to defend. In turning away from religion it does not seek to glorify humanity. It has no room for naive talk of 'the religion of humanity' which some nineteenth-century secularists tried to substitute for Christianity. It involves no claims about the inevitability of progress. If it includes a commitment to human rationality, that is not a belief that reason will necessarily triumph, or that human beings can be relied on to act rationally provided only that the influence of those who have a vested interest in keeping us in ignorance can be kept at bay. In the wake of Darwin and Marx and Freud we know how strong are the irrational forces of biological instincts, collective ideologies, and repressed desires. The fact remains, however, that we do also possess distinctively human capacities for rational thought and action, and that we should use them as best we can, along with our equally human capacities for love and care and compassion, to resist the cruelty and the inhumanity which led to the concentration camps.

The humanism which I want to defend is not a naive faith in the essential goodness of human beings, but on the other hand it is not an attitude of bleak pessimistic despair. It makes little sense to talk of human beings either as naturally good or as inherently corrupt and evil. We know the terrible things which human beings are capable of doing in certain conditions. We know also the acts of heroism, the struggles for social justice, the artistic and creative achievements of which some human beings have been capable, sometimes indeed inspired by a religious faith but often inspired simply by a commitment to their fellow human beings and by a desire to make the fullest use of their human potentialities.

My definition of humanism is a personal one. There is no humanist creed, no set of beliefs to which every humanist has to subscribe. Humanism is not a dogma or a sect. Nevertheless I believe that the humanism which I want to defend is one which others share. I shall seek to show that the things which we value in human life are not an illusion; that as human beings we can find from our own resources the shared moral values which we need in order to live together, and the means to create meaningful and fulfilling lives for ourselves; and that the rejection of religious belief need not be a cause for despair.

Two

I have said that the starting point for secular humanism is the rejection of religious belief, and that is where I shall start. I shall look first, very briefly, at the traditional classic arguments for the existence of a god. There is an enormous literature dealing with them, and what I have to say will be perfunctory and will not add anything new, but it is an integral part of my case for humanism and I need to say it. Many modern religious believers and many theologians tend to dismiss these traditional arguments. Of course, they say, no one now relies on them; it is accepted that religious belief cannot be based simply on rational argument, and has to be understood in quite different terms. I shall be looking later at these alternative readings of religious belief, all of which seem to me to be woefully inadequate. The only intellectually honest version of religious belief, in my view, is one which does attempt to support it with reasons and evidence. I am also inclined to think that such arguments play more of a role in the religious thinking of ordinary people than trendy theologians recognise. My mother, who became rather religious in the last years of her life, loved feeding the birds in her garden, and she used to look at them with admiration and say to me, 'I know you don't agree with me, but there must be something that started it all.' Her remark is a sort of cross between what we shall now consider under the labels of 'the first cause argument' and 'the argument from design', and I suspect that ideas of this kind play a significant part in the thinking of many believers.

ARGUMENTS FOR THE EXISTENCE OF GOD

The traditional arguments are standardly listed as the *ontological* argument, the *cosmological* argument, and the *teleological* argument. The second and third of these are serious arguments, the first is bizarre, but for the sake of completeness I shall briefly mention the ontological argument. It goes like this:

> God is, by definition, the most perfect being of which we can conceive.
>
> But a god which did not exist would not be perfect, since we could conceive of a greater being, one which had all the same attributes plus that of existence.
>
> Therefore a perfect being must have existence as one of its attributes.
>
> Therefore God, being a perfect being, must exist.

From a purely academic point of view the argument is an intriguing one, but it is pretty clear that there is something fishy about it. Philosophers have argued for centuries about precisely how to pin down what is wrong with it. I shall not go into the controversies here. For our present purposes it is sufficient to say that the existence of God cannot just be a matter of definition. Whether or not there is a god is a substantive factual question about the nature of reality, and we cannot settle it simply by defining God into existence with a verbal sleight of hand.

The second traditional argument is the cosmological argument. This employs the idea of God as the so-called 'first cause' of everything else that exists. The term 'first cause' can be interpreted to mean either first in time, or first in the sense that it is the ultimate cause of everything else which exists and is itself uncaused by anything else. In either case the argument has the same basic logical structure:

> Everything in the natural world is caused by something else, which in turn is caused by something else again.
> But this sequence of prior causes cannot be infinite.
> Therefore there must be a first cause which is the ultimate cause of everything that exists.
> This first cause is God.

There are two basic problems with this argument. If we understand 'first cause' to mean 'first in time', it is not clear why there has to be a first cause in this sense. Why could there not be an infinite series of causes with no beginning? Admittedly we find this idea of an infinite sequence in infinite time hard to grasp, but it is no less implausible than the idea of an entity which began the causal chain, was not itself caused by anything else, and therefore itself either came into existence uncaused, or had existed from all eternity. That is just as puzzling as the idea of an infinite series of causes with no beginning. And if we understand 'first cause' to mean not 'first in time' but 'the ultimate cause of everything else', it is even less clear why there has to be a first cause. Why cannot the universe consist of entities which all interact causally with one another but no one of which is the cause of all the rest?

That, in either of its versions, is the first problem with the argument. The second problem is that in any case, even if there were such an entity, something which was a first cause either in the sense of being first in time or in the sense of being an ultimate cause not itself caused by anything else, why should it be a god? Why not identify this ultimate cause with the universe itself, or matter, or physical energy?

Attempts to answer that challenge are likely to lead us to the third traditional argument, the teleological argument, also known as 'the argument from design'. The nature of the universe, it may be said, is such that its ultimate cause cannot be a purely physical or mechanical cause. Innumerable items in the universe give the appearance of being *adapted to a purpose*, and the best explanation for why they have the nature which they have is that their features all serve a purpose. The universe, in other words, provides abundant evidence of intelligent design, and the ultimate explanation for such a universe must therefore be that it was created by an intelligent designer.

This seems to me to be by far the most plausible of the traditional arguments, and it is one which we must take seriously. The most famous formulation of it was provided by William Paley in his book *Natural Theology* published in 1802. Paley's first example of design in nature is that of the eye:

I know no better method of introducing so large a subject, than that of comparing a single thing with a single thing; an eye, for example, with a telescope. As far as the examination of the instrument goes, there is precisely the same proof that the eye was made for vision, as there is that the telescope was made for assisting it. They are made upon the same principles; both being adjusted to the laws by which the transmission and refraction of rays of light are regulated. . . . For instance; these laws require, in order to produce the same effect, that the rays of light, in passing from water into the eye, should be refracted by a more convex surface, than when it passes out of air into the eye. Accordingly we find that the eye of a fish, in that part of it called the crystalline lens, is much rounder than the eye of terrestrial animals. What plainer manifestation of design can there be than this difference?[1]

Paley continues at great length to enumerate all the other features of the eye which manifest this same character of design for a purpose, and this, he argues, is just one of innumerable examples, throughout the organic world, of purposive adaptation which can only be explained by intentional contrivance on the part of a divine creator.

There is indeed something here which needs to be explained. The question is whether the hypothesis of a divine designer is the best explanation, and that depends in part on what alternative explanation there might be. Paley recognises the form that an alternative explanation might take. It

would persuade us to believe, that the eye, the animal to which it belongs, every other animal, every plant, indeed every organized body which we see, are only so many out of the possible varieties and combinations of being, which the lapse of infinite ages has brought into existence; that the present world is the relict of that variety; millions of other bodily forms and other species having perished, being by the defect of their constitution incapable of preservation, or of continuance by generation.[2]

This is a form of explanation first offered by some of the ancient Greek philosophers such as Empedocles and the atomists. Paley regards any such explanation as implausible. There is no evidence of such processes going on in nature, he says, and in any case how could mere chance produce such abundant appearances of design? The question is, then, whether this form of explanation can be made plausible. I think that it can be. The plausible version of it is Darwinian evolutionary theory, and I subscribe to the widely held view that Darwin has, in effect, refuted the argument from design. The scientific explanation has supplanted the theistic explanation. I want to dwell on this point for a while, because it raises some important issues about the relation between humanism and science. The idea of an alliance between the two has been a central strand in the humanist tradition, and I think that the idea is essentially right, but I do not just want to appeal uncritically to the authority and prestige of science. In our contemporary culture too many people are content to say 'Scientists have shown that . . .', but the appeal to the authority of scientists, if it is simply an appeal to authority, is as inadequate as is the appeal to religious authority. Why should we accept the scientific explanation of apparent design in nature, and where does it leave the theistic explanation? Attention to these questions will help us to get clear about the relation between humanism and science.

Most intelligent religious believers now accept Darwinian evolutionary theory. They would say that it is consistent with the argument from design, and that it complements explanations in terms of divine agency. I shall move on to consider that position later, but first let us look at the simple opposition between Darwinism and the theory of 'separate creation' – the idea that each species of living thing was directly created by divine agency. The extreme version of so-called 'creationism' is the biblical fundamentalism which accepts the account of creation in the opening chapter of the Bible as literal truth – the universe was directly created by God, a few thousand years ago, over a period of six days, including the heavens and the earth and all the species of plants and animals which at present inhabit the earth. I take it to be quite certain that

Darwinian theory provides a much better explanation of the origin of species and their purposive adaptation than does biblical literalism. Why is this?

DARWIN AND EVOLUTION

Note first that Darwin's innovation was not the theory of evolution as such. I have already mentioned that ideas of evolution were first explored by the ancient Greek philosophers. In Darwin's day they were again in the air, and he began *The Origin of Species* (first published in 1859) with a review of current evolutionary ideas including those of his grandfather Erasmus Darwin, Jean Baptiste Lamarck, Isidore Geoffroy Saint-Hilaire, Herbert Spencer, and the anonymous author of an influential work called *Vestiges of Creation* published in 1844. In geology it was already widely accepted that the earth was millions of years older than was indicated by any literal reading of the Bible, that the different kinds of rocks could be explained in terms of the gradual laying down of geological strata, over very long periods of time, by processes which were still continuing, and that the geological data included the fossilised remains of different species located in different geological layers. The fossil evidence, however, is not by itself sufficient to establish evolutionary theory. It is consistent with the separate creation of different species. To make the evolutionary hypothesis plausible, what was needed was a convincing account of the *mechanism* by which one species could have evolved into another. This was Darwin's distinctive contribution – the mechanism of 'natural selection'.

The theory of natural selection is now accepted by all reputable biologists, but as I have said, I do not wish simply to appeal to the authority of science. That would be as unthinking and as inadequate as appeals to revelation to establish the truths of religion. Although those of us who are not experts cannot appreciate the detailed evidence, the case for evolution through natural selection is a case which anyone can understand, and it was set out with the utmost clarity by Darwin himself. The concluding chapter of *The Origin of Species*, in which he summarises his case, should be obligatory reading for any educated person, and I am going to quote some paragraphs from it in order to present Darwin's own argument in his own words. The core argument takes the form of an analogy between the breeding of domesticated plants and animals and the process of natural selection.

1 Selection and breeding of domestic varieties

Darwin first refers us to the familiar fact of the breeding of domesticated plant and animal species. Variations which occur naturally in domesticated species can be selected to suit the purposes of the breeder, the modifications are inherited by successive generations, and successive small variations can be accumulated over many generations to produce, say, a new breed of sheep or a new variety of rose.

Variability is not actually caused by man. . . . But man can and does select the variations given him by nature, and thus accumulates them in any desired manner. He thus adapts animals and plants for his own benefit or pleasure. . . . It is certain that he can largely influence the character of a breed by selecting, in each successive generation, individual differences so slight as to be inappreciable except by an educated eye. This unconscious process of selection has been the great agency in the formation of the most distinct and useful domestic breeds. That many breeds produced by man have to a large extent the character of natural species, is shown by the inextricable doubts whether many of them are varieties or aboriginally distinct species.[3]

2 Variation under nature and natural selection

Darwin then argues that the same process takes place within nature as under domesticated conditions, and that what he calls 'the struggle for existence' functions as a mechanism of selection comparable to selection and breeding by human beings.

> There is no reason why the principles which have acted so efficiently under domestication should not have acted under nature. In the survival of favoured individuals and races, during the constantly-recurrent Struggle for Existence, we see a powerful and ever-acting form of Selection. . . . More individuals are born than can possibly survive. A grain in the balance may determine which individuals shall live and which shall die, – which variety or species shall increase in number, and which shall decrease or finally become extinct. . . . The slightest advantage in certain individuals . . . over those with which they come into competition, or better adaptation in however slight a degree to the surrounding physical conditions, will, in the long run, turn the balance.[4]

3 From varieties to species

There is no clear divide between 'varieties' and 'species', and the gradual accumulation of modifications can produce changes which are not just new varieties but new species.

> It has often been asserted, but the assertion is incapable of proof, that the amount of variation under nature is a strictly limited quantity. Man . . . can produce within a short period a great result by adding up mere individual differences in

his domestic productions; and every one admits that species present individual differences. But, besides such differences, all naturalists admit that natural varieties exist, which are considered sufficiently distinct to be worthy of record in systematic works. No one has drawn any clear distinction between individual differences and slight varieties; or between more plainly marked varieties and sub-species, and species. On separate continents, and on different parts of the same continent when divided by barriers of any kind, and on outlying islands, what a multitude of forms exist, which some experienced naturalists rank as varieties, others as geographical races or sub-species, and others as distinct, though closely allied species![5]

4 Conclusion

This process, continued over vast periods of time, is sufficient to account for the gradual emergence of all the species of living things which have existed.

If then, animals and plants do vary, let it be ever so slightly and slowly, why should not variation or individual differences, which are in any way beneficial, be preserved and accumulated by natural selection, or the survival of the fittest? If man can by patience select variations useful to him, why, under changing and complex conditions of life, should not variations useful to nature's living products often arise, and be preserved or selected? What limits can be put to this power, acting during long ages and rigidly scrutinising the whole constitution, structure, and habits of each creature, – favouring the good and rejecting the bad? I can see no limit to this power, in slowly and beautifully adapting each form to the most complex relations of life. The theory of natural selection, even if we look no farther than this, seems to be in the highest degree probable.[6]

To summarise, then:

1 We know that artificial selection of domesticated plants and animals can produce new varieties.
2 We know that an analogous process of natural selection takes place in nature to produce new varieties better adapted to their environment.
3 There is no reason why the process of natural selection which produces new varieties may not, over sufficiently long periods of time, also produce varieties so different as to constitute new species.
4 The mechanism of natural selection can therefore explain how new species have come into existence with features adapted to their environment.

I have said that the form of this argument is an argument from analogy, the analogy between domestic breeding and natural selection. The argument from design is also an argument from analogy, and it too purports to specify a mechanism by which species and their purposive adaptation come about, so we need to compare the two explanations in these respects. Here is the design argument formulated to emphasise the analogy on which it rests:

1 Living things and other features of the natural world are organised in such a way that they serve a purpose.
2 Where human artefacts are organised in such a way that they serve a purpose, this is because they have been created by an intelligent designer.
3 Therefore those features of the natural world which are

organised to serve a purpose must also have been created by an intelligent designer.

The analogy does have some initial plausibility. We know what it is for a craftsman to make something, for a carpenter to make a chair so that people can sit comfortably in it, or for an architect to design a house in such a way that the walls stand up and the roof stays on and people can live in it. In the absence of anything better, then, the hypothesis of intelligent design by a divine craftsman provides an analogy with something familiar and understandable, and that is what has given the explanation its initial appeal. The trouble is that we have no idea how to fill in the details of the explanation. We cannot specify any of the physical processes, comparable to the carpenter's cutting and shaping of the wood, or the builder's assembling of the bricks and mortar. However powerful we may suppose the divine creator to be, we have no idea what physical techniques he might use, analogous to those of the human craftsman, to create something as vast and intricate as the natural world. (Actually we do have one idea, but I will come back to that shortly.) And if it is said, as it will be, that God is not a physical being but an infinitely powerful and omniscient mind who can create the universe by an exercise of intelligent will, then we have even less idea how a disembodied mind could, simply by thinking and willing, create a physical world and act on it, just as we have no idea how a craftsman could create a chair or a house simply by thinking about it.

'Of course we can't understand it,' it may be said, 'we're talking about something which is way beyond our human comprehension and which must remain a mystery.' But then that's just the trouble – we no longer have an explanation. An argument by analogy, such as the argument from design, is only as good as the analogy on which it rests. If the analogy is a weak analogy, then the argument is a weak argument. The analogy in this case is a weak analogy, because we have no way of filling in the details. In contrast, the Darwinian explanation works because it invokes familiar processes, of biological reproduction and inheritance, natural variation, and the struggle for survival, and it shows how, given a sufficient time-span, these mechanisms can account for the emergence of species adapted to their environment and possessing physical organs adapted to their functions. And the experimental biosciences, including modern genetics, can fill out, in immense detail, the picture of how these mechanisms work and how they can explain the origin of species.

Many would say that in using Darwin as a stick with which to beat the argument from design, I am attacking a straw man. As I have acknowledged, most intelligent theists these days accept Darwinian evolution and regard it as consistent with religious belief. I said just now that the explanation of purposive adaptation in nature which invokes a divine creator fails because it cannot fill in the details, it cannot specify the mechanisms by which this creative process is carried out. Yes it can, the theist may say, the required mechanism is the process of evolution through natural selection. That is how the design is implemented, and that is why the theist can welcome Darwin with open arms.

That's fine. The position is indeed a perfectly consistent one, and it tells us something important about the relation between religion and science. Darwinian theory does not *refute* religious belief. It does not prove that there is no god. If we have good independent reasons for believing in a god, we can indeed combine that belief with the acceptance of the scientific theory of evolution through natural selection. What the scientific theory does, however, is to undermine fatally the argument from design. It establishes that we do not need to posit a divine creator in order to explain the intricacies of living things and their apparent design. And if, as I think, the argument from design is the only plausible argument for the existence of a god, then religious belief no longer has a rational basis.

Yes it does, the reply may come, because the scientific explanation still leaves something further to be explained. We can explain the present existence of plants and animals adapted to their environment by referring to a long process of evolution over many millions of years, and we can explain in the same way how the most rudimentary forms of life originated as chance combinations of chemicals, but we still have to explain why there exists, in the first place, a physical universe constituted in that way, with the causal conditions to make that long and complicated process possible.[7]

Here we are back with something like the first cause argument, and as before it is not clear to me either that there is anything to be explained here, or that belief in a god is capable of doing any explaining. We can explain some features of the universe, such as purposive adaptation, in terms of other things which caused them, but all explanations have to come to an end somewhere with certain features of the universe which we have to accept as a matter of brute fact. If theists claim to explain the existence of the universe by saying that God willed it to exist, they are no better off, since they can give no answer to the question 'Why is there a god?' This is the brute fact of existence which they simply have to accept.

I conclude that the attempts to provide rational arguments for the existence of God fail. As with the particular case of the failure of the argument from design, this does not prove that there is no god. Someone may come up with a new argument, or a new piece of evidence. I doubt it, after all this time, but it is not impossible. The fact remains, however, that the onus is on the theists to produce a good reason for thinking that there is a god, and if those reasons are not forthcoming, then so much the worse for religious belief.

REVELATION, RELIGIOUS EXPERIENCE, AND FAITH

Am I putting too much weight on rational argument? Many religious believers would say that I am. These traditional arguments for the existence of God are outmoded, they would say; no one now thinks that you can be reasoned into a belief in God by means of arguments. For myself I think that the retreat from reason on the part of theists is a wholly retrograde step. I have every respect for those theists who are prepared to enter into the argument, to give their reasons and to respond to criticisms. I am not persuaded by them, but they have a case to make and it deserves to be heard. If, on the other hand, religious believers offer no rational arguments in support of their beliefs, why should we take them seriously? Nevertheless, let us look at some of the suggested alternatives to rational argument and see what they amount to.

One of them is the appeal to revelation. 'We know that there is a god, because he has revealed himself to us through his prophets, and through his own words in the holy book' – the Bible, the Qur'an, or whatever. This as it stands is hopeless. If we *already* had independent reasons for believing that there is a god, then we could go on to look for further reasons why this or that particular individual or particular book might be an authentic conveyor of his words. But these claimed revelations cannot be the basis for our belief in God in the first place. To say 'We know that God exists, because he has told us that he does' is blatantly circular.

If this approach has anything going for it, that can only be because it merges into a second supposed alternative to rational argument – the appeal to direct experience. Revelation may be a basis for belief if it takes the form not of an appeal to the authority of a self-proclaimed prophet or holy book, but of a revelation which one has oneself received as a personal experience. The supposed religious experience can take various forms. It might be a matter of literally hearing a voice or seeing a vision. It might be some kind of mystical experience – a sense of being at one with the universe, or detached from time, or at peace with the world. Experiences of this latter kind merge with a third category, that of various kinds of emotional experience such as having someone to turn to in times of trouble and feeling that one is being given support from a source outside oneself.

This is a mixed bag of experiences and it brings with it a mixed bag of problems. First, experiences always have to be interpreted. They do not come ready-labelled. There are no experiences which are self-authenticating in the sense of carrying with them a guarantee of what it is that they are experiences of. If I think I hear voices, it may be the wind in the trees, it may be the product of my imagination or of my fraught emotional condition, or it may be God speaking to me. Moses thought that he saw God in a burning bush; others would say that he just saw a burning bush. We have to interpret these experiences in the light of our understanding of the rest of the world and the probabilities of the various possible explanations. The interpretation of the experience as hearing the voice of God will be the most probable explanation only if we have reliable independent grounds for believing that there is a god who regularly communicates with human beings in this way. One such experience cannot by itself be a reliable basis for such a belief.

A second problem is the inherent vagueness of many supposed religious experiences, especially those of the 'mystical' kind. A feeling of being at one with the universe may be very pleasant and uplifting, but the only religious beliefs which it can support will themselves be of the vaguest kind. It is a huge leap from such experiences to anything which could meaningfully be called a belief in the existence of a god – an intelligent living being who exercises some kind of control over the universe. The gap cannot be bridged without a thorough and rigorous *argument*.

A third problem with the appeal to direct experience is that many of the experiences in question, especially those of the emotional kind, can much more plausibly be explained in terms of wishful thinking. It is very comforting, in times of trouble, to feel that one's life is in the hands of a loving and omnipotent god, but, precisely because it is comforting, we should be sceptical of basing any beliefs on such a feeling. I do not deny that a sense of being able to rely on supernatural comfort and support may meet an overwhelming need. It may be that people sometimes cannot cope without such a belief, and I would not want to deprive them of that support, but the fact that the belief meets a need does not make it true.

So much for the appeals to revelation and to direct religious experience. The most extreme form of the rejection of rational argument consists in setting up 'faith' as the alternative to 'reason'. It is difficult to know exactly what is meant by this, and I am not sure that there is a coherent position here at all. Sometimes it looks like a reformulation of the appeal to direct experience of the emotional kind; drawing on the connotations of 'faith' as 'trust', believers sometimes say that faith in God is trust in a saviour who is always there to offer strength and support. Like trust in a friend or in a parent, it does not need to be backed up by reasons but is rather the expression of a direct interpersonal relationship. I do not think that this analogy can take us very far. In the cases of trust in a friend or a parent, we have plenty of evidence that the other person exists, and the trust which we place in them is not a substitute for that. But if there are no independent reasons for thinking that the god in whom we place our trust actually exists, then faith in him is more like a child's trust in Father Christmas or in an imaginary 'special friend'.

If the appeal to faith is not in some way allied to evidence or reasons, if it is simply a refusal to countenance any reasons at all, then it is impossible to refute and impossible to argue with, but that is because it is in the end making no claim to truth at all. Someone who says 'My belief in God is not something for which I can give any reasons, it is simply a matter of faith, and reasons are irrelevant' is in effect break-ing off communication. To put forward a belief as true is to offer it as a belief which others can share and endorse, and thus to imply that there are considerations which count as reasons for others to hold the belief, even if they do not in fact recognise them as such. Conversely, to say that there are literally *no* reasons which others could have for sharing and adopting one's belief is to forfeit any claim to the truth of the belief.

The appeal to faith is sometimes bolstered by the claim that *all* beliefs ultimately rest on a non-rational faith. To illustrate this claim we can usefully consider again the controversy about *creationism*, to which I have already referred. Creationism is the view that the creation story in the first chapter of the

Bible is literally true, that the whole universe, including our own earth with its species of plants and animals and the first human beings, was created by the direct agency of God in a period of six days, a few thousand years ago, and that the scientifically accepted theories of the origin of the universe, of the solar system, and of the gradual emergence of living species through the process of evolution over millions of years, are mistaken. Creationism has a large following in the United States, and though it has less support in Britain there has recently been controversy over the teaching of it in some British schools. The arguments offered by creationists often purport to be scientific arguments. They point to what they see as difficulties for evolutionary theory, such as gaps in the fossil record, or the alleged circularity of dating geological strata on the basis of fossil remains found in them and at the same time citing the geological record as evidence for evolutionary theory. Creationists claim that the theory of direct creation can equally well account for the fossil record. They suggest, for instance, that the layers of rocks with different levels of fossil remains could have been produced by some relatively recent abrupt upheaval such as the great flood described in *Genesis*. They may claim that creationism provides a *better* explanation of the available evidence, but they also rely on another move: that since we have two conflicting theories each of which can be made consistent with the evidence, acceptance of evolutionary theory is as much of a 'faith position' as is acceptance of creationism, and the biblical fundamentalist who opts for the latter is therefore being no less rational than the believer in evolution.

There are more sophisticated versions of this kind of position which do not have any connection with creationism but do similarly question the status of science. There are thinkers of a 'postmodernist' persuasion, for instance, who say that there is no such thing as 'knowledge' in general, there are only different 'knowledges', and there is therefore no reason to think that scientific method has any privileged status as the most reliable route to knowledge. These different 'knowledges' are sometimes said to be 'constructions', creative fictions rather than attempts to reflect an independent and objective reality. They are sometimes referred to as alternative 'discourses', different languages which are all equally legitimate and no one of which can be said to be uniquely correct. Or, borrowing a term from the later philosophy of Wittgenstein, they are said to be different 'language-games'. There is no 'grand narrative', it is said, which can stand above these competing discourses and legitimate the special status of science. Science is thus reduced to the status of one language-game among others, a self-contained discourse with its own rules, self-legitimating but incapable of legitimating other language-games or being legitimated by them.[8]

There are troubling questions here, not least for humanists, who have traditionally championed science as the rival to the claims of religion. Why should we accept what 'science' tells us? It is a question by which we ought to be troubled, for the social prestige of science leads all too often to the acceptance of scientific knowledge on the basis of an appeal to authority. Most people are not scientists, and can give no better reason for accepting, say, the theory of evolution or the 'Big Bang' theory of cosmology, or any other scientific theory, than that it is what 'scientists have shown'. Is science then in danger of becoming a new religion, with its own priesthood whose utterances are accepted unquestioningly?

THE STATUS OF SCIENCE

Let us continue with the example of Darwinian evolutionary theory. Why should we accept it? It is not good enough just to appeal to authority, to say 'It must be right because it is now universally accepted by all reputable biologists.' We do have to acknowledge, however, that, in this as in all areas of our lives, knowledge is impossible unless we take a great deal of it on trust from others who are in a better position to know. Here are some randomly chosen examples of the innumerable beliefs which I hold, scientific and non-scientific, which I cannot check for myself but which I accept on what I take to be reliable authority:

> There is no intelligent life on Mars.
>
> The earth's rain-forests are disappearing at an increasing rate.
>
> Bach's B-minor Mass was never performed as a complete work in his lifetime.
>
> It is impossible to determine simultaneously the location and velocity of a sub-atomic particle.

To vindicate any kind of knowledge, then, we need some understanding of what counts as good grounds for rational trust. In the case of the specialist sciences, that trust has to be a trust in certain kinds of institutions. We know that the scientific community is one in which scientists are in a position to check the claimed results of their colleagues. We rely on them to do so because as non-scientists we know something of the way in which scientific results are published and disseminated through conferences and academic journals, and of the processes of refereeing and peer review by which scientists, like scholars in other disciplines, assess the work of their colleagues. And our awareness of and trust in these procedures must stem from our own involvement in academic and educational institutions, whether as practitioners or as students (a point which has significant implications for the purposes of a national system of education).

Trust in institutional procedures is important, then, but it is not enough. Our trust of scientists and other specialists is not sufficiently rational unless it is also based on some understanding of the methods they employ, of the ways in which scientific theories are tested and the evidence which is needed to support them. The standard account is that scientific theories are tested by experience, and that this means by observation and experiment. How does this apply to evolutionary theory? There are obvious problems here, for the theory cannot be directly tested. It is not possible to rerun in a laboratory a developmental process which has taken millions of years. We cannot engineer genetic mutations, test them in the appropriate environments and see whether they confer advantages which facilitate survival and whether they are then inherited and become dominant. This is a serious point which should properly induce a certain degree of scepticism towards some of the more dogmatic pronouncements of some Darwinian popularisers. When they confidently tell us that this or that trait of human beings or of any other species (say, for example, sexual fidelity in women or sexual infidelity in men) served a certain purpose and that this explains why the species has this trait, we have to recognise that such claims cannot be directly tested and confirmed, and are in that sense speculative. We can try to ascertain the details of the environment in which the trait emerged, and then imagine what advantages it *would have* conferred, but we still have the problem of counter-factuals: though we know that the species possessing this trait did in fact survive, we cannot directly ascertain whether or not it would have survived if it had *not* possessed this trait. Thus we cannot directly test the causal relationship between the features of the environment, the survival value of a particular trait, and the persistence of that trait. Still less, then, can we directly test the overall theory which explains in terms of such causal relationships the origins of all living species.

If the theory is in this sense speculative, does that after all make it a 'faith position'? To rebut this charge we need to show how the theory is still anchored in experience. The relation between the theory and the empirical evidence may be less than straightforward, but if it is not at some point tied to experience it becomes a free-floating construct and we can then pick and choose theories simply to suit our fancy. Creationism, astrology, alchemy and serious scientific theories will all be on equal terms.

Let us recall the empirical evidence which Darwin himself drew on to support the theory of natural selection. The relevant empirical claims are:

1 In domesticated conditions, variations in plants and animals can be accumulated by selection.
2 Variations occur in natural species.
3 There is no sharp divide between varieties, sub-species, and species.
4 More organisms are produced than can survive.

From 4 it follows that individuals with variations which provide them with advantages in their particular habitat are more likely to survive and reproduce. Taken together with empirical claims 1, 2 and 3, this provides a *possible* explanation of the origin of natural species, but only if we postulate an extremely long time-scale over which the small variations can be accumulated. What evidence is there for such a time-scale? There is the geological evidence. The layers of different kinds of rocks are best explained in terms of familiar geological processes extended over vast periods of time. The geological evidence not only supports the time-scale, but also supports the evolutionary theory by linking different species with different levels and dating the most rudimentary life-forms to the oldest geological strata. Now that evidence is in itself consistent with the separate creation of different species. It may help to establish which species came into existence in which geological periods, but it does not yet establish that later species *evolved from* earlier ones. However, the evolutionary hypothesis becomes more compelling when the geological evidence is brought together with the theory of natural selection, because the latter identifies a *mechanism* which explains *how* new species could have evolved from earlier ones. It thus strengthens the explanation which the geological evidence cannot by itself confirm. (Prior to the publication of *The Origin of Species* and Darwin's identification of the mechanism of natural selection, evolutionary theories, though widely advocated, were not firmly established, and were rejected by some of the most eminent geologists.)

So now, with the combination of the geological evidence and the mechanism of natural selection, we have a plausible explanation of the origin of living species, backed by empirical evidence. As we have seen, however, other explanations are also compatible with the evidence, and in particular, creationism can be made consistent with it. It is not logically contradictory to suppose that the entire universe was created

6,000 years ago, complete with the galaxies exactly as modern astrophysics supposes them to have been at that time, with the geological strata just as they are, containing the fossil record just as we find it. Although the astrophysics strongly suggests an expanding universe whose expansion has been going on for millions of years, and although the geological evidence strongly suggests a sequence of the emergence of new species over vast periods of time, why cannot the creationists stick to their claim that such a universe was created by God in six days in 4004 BC? Why should we accept evolutionary theory as the correct explanation of the empirical evidence, rather than the creationist explanation which is also logically consistent with the evidence?

Notice first that the creationist account can be made consistent with the evidence only by inventing *ad hoc* hypotheses to explain it.[9] By '*ad hoc*' I mean new hypotheses which have to be conjured up from somewhere for each particular problem. For instance, the creationists may explain the fossil evidence by suggesting that perhaps there was a great flood which covered the whole of the earth's surface and that the most rudimentary life-forms sank to the bottom but the most complex living things were able to struggle to the top. That is a *possible* explanation of the distribution of fossils in the geological strata, but it is not an explanation which is embedded in any larger, more comprehensive theory. Evolutionary theory, we can say by contrast, is a good explanation of this and innumerable other phenomena, because it is *economical*. It provides a single overall perspective which can be applied in a systematic way to a diversity of empirical phenomena.

We need to be clear about what we mean by 'economy' here. The creationist explanation is a simple one. What indeed could be simpler than the idea that the whole universe, including our earth with its innumerable species of plants and animals, was created by an all-powerful God, and that we can explain anything simply by saying that it is as it is because God willed it to be so? *Economy*, however, is not the same thing as simplicity. An economical theory is one which provides a perspective which can be applied in a systematic way to generate detailed explanations of a diversity of empirical phenomena. The detail is important. The appeal to the power of a creator god does not provide that detail, it merely gives the same general explanation for everything. It has simplicity but not economy.

A theory is also more economical if it brings together different areas of scientific enquiry. Newtonian physics, for example, provided a more powerful explanatory framework than the physics which it replaced partly because it was able to bring together astronomical and terrestrial phenomena and apply the same scientific laws to both. Physics in the Aristotelian tradition had to provide different kinds of explanations for the movements of the heavenly bodies and the movements of physical bodies on earth, whereas both sets of phenomena could be explained by the Newtonian laws of motion and gravitational theory. In the same way, as we have seen, Darwinian theory brought together the geological phenomena, including the study of fossils, with knowledge of the domestic breeding of plants and animals, and this in turn with the well-established biological facts about the behaviour of living organisms in their environments which Darwin referred to as 'the struggle for existence'. This capacity of a theoretical perspective to bring together different spheres of enquiry within a single unifying theory is sometimes referred to as 'consilience'. A further instance of this, since Darwin's time, has been the so-called neo-Darwinian synthesis. Darwin himself had no clear conception of how new variations of plants and animals could come about and could be inherited. That understanding has now been provided by modern genetics, which was pioneered by Mendel and has been enormously enhanced by the discovery of the chemical constitution and structure of the genetic template in the twentieth century. This synthesis of evolutionary theory with the modern science of genetics is a further example of consilience and it has added enormously to the economy and explanatory power of the theory.

The synthesis of evolutionary theory with modern genetics also draws our attention to two other features of a good explanation. The first is the fertility of a theory – its capacity to generate a detailed research programme. Day-to-day scientific research is concerned not to devise revolutionary new large-scale theories, but to apply established theoretical perspectives to a mass of detailed empirical data. Thus modern genetics has led to detailed research into the sequencing of the DNA of different organisms, including the Human Genome Project, the research project to map the entire genetic code of human beings. The overall theory poses a mass of detailed questions about the coding and function of the chromosomes which make up the human genome, and proposes the research methods for answering those questions, and each success in answering them provides further confirmation of the theory.

In the case of genetics, including the Human Genome Project, the answers have important practical implications. Understanding the genetic structure of non-human plants and animals makes it possible to produce genetically modified crops, or to clone domesticated animals. Identifying the genetic mutations which cause diseases such as muscular dystrophy or cystic fibrosis makes it possible to screen for such diseases, and to look for forms of genetic therapy. All these developments are controversial, of course, and I am not now taking a view on whether or not they are to be welcomed, but I am suggesting that insofar as we acknowledge the practical and ethical questions we are acknowledging the success of the scientific theory which makes these practical developments possible. This brings us to the other feature of a good scientific theory: its *practical applicability*. The success of modern science is built into the world in which we live. Every time we drive a car, or cross a bridge, or fly in an aeroplane, or switch on the electric light, or send an e-mail, we provide ourselves with further confirmation of the success of the scientific theories which have generated these practical applications. Our trust in scientific method does not have to be a blind faith in the authority of scientists; it can be a rational trust based on our awareness of and reliance on the fruits of modern science which we see all around us.

A good scientific theory, then, is one which is consistent with and can explain the *empirical data*, which is *economical* in the sense of bringing a mass of detailed phenomena within a unifying framework, which is *fertile* in the sense of generating an ongoing programme of detailed further research, and whose *practical applications* provide innumerable successful tests of the theory which can be recognised by specialists and lay-persons alike. Our trust in the methods of science, unlike trust in religious authority and revelation, is a rational trust, and the upshot of this chapter is therefore to reaffirm a rather old-fashioned view about the relation between religion and science: that the growth of modern science has undermined the credentials of religion. I am not asserting that religion and science are necessarily in conflict. My claim is the more complex one which can be put in the form of a dilemma.

Either (a) religious beliefs are interpreted and applied in such a way as to bring them into *conflict* with scientific theories, in which case we have good reasons for accepting the scientific theories and rejecting the religious beliefs;

or (b) religious beliefs are interpreted and applied in such a way as to make them *consistent* with accepted scientific theories, in which case the religious beliefs are redundant and do not explain anything which cannot be better explained by the scientific theories.

The former position is taken by the creationists and other religious fundamentalists, and in opposition to them I have argued that our acceptance of established scientific theories is rational and well-founded, whereas there is no good reason why we should accept beliefs which are based on an appeal to divine revelation and which are in conflict with scientific knowledge. The second position is the one taken by more sophisticated contemporary religious believers. It is perfectly possible to reconcile science and religion in this way. It is quite consistent to maintain both that the origins of the universe, of our earth and of living species can be explained by the established scientific theories and that these theories can be read as accounts of the workings of a divine creator. The problem with this position is that there is no good reason to add the latter claim. The religious component of such a hybrid position cannot be refuted, but there is no good reason why we should endorse it. We cannot appeal to arguments such as the 'first cause' argument or the argument from design to show that a belief in a god is needed to explain the existence and nature of the universe, since it is acknowledged that these can be satisfactorily explained in scientific terms. And as I have indicated in this chapter, if we cannot appeal to rational arguments to establish the existence of a deity, there is nothing else which will fill the gap. Religious belief is not refuted, but it simply collapses for lack of a foundation.

As we shall see in the next three chapters, I am not suggesting that science has all the answers, or that scientific understanding is the only kind of understanding which we need. There are philosophical questions, ethical questions, and questions about the meaning we give to our lives, which science cannot answer – not because the credentials of scientific knowledge are in any way insecure, but simply because the questions are not scientific questions. I turn now to the consideration of these questions, and of the answers which a humanist might give to them.

Why science undermines religion

Three

One of the criticisms frequently made of atheistic humanism, especially by people of a religious persuasion, is that it embraces a diminished conception of what it is to be human. Especially because of its alliance with a scientific view of the world, it is said to be committed to something called 'materialism' and therefore to leave no room for what makes us distinctively human – our 'higher' nature, our 'soul' or 'spirit' in virtue of which we are 'made in the image of God'. What are we to make of these charges?

MATERIALISM

We had better note first the extremely loose and confusing way in which the word 'materialism' is often used in this context. The criticisms just mentioned regularly trade on an elementary ambiguity in the use of the word. 'Materialism' is sometimes used to refer to a view about values – roughly speaking, the view that the only things worth living for are 'material goods', that is, money and the consumer goods that money can buy. In the next chapter I shall turn to the question of humanist values, but for now it is enough to say that there is absolutely no reason why humanists should be committed to 'materialism' in this sense. And though vast numbers of people, including many who would call themselves religious, in practice live as though they embraced materialism, it is not a view which any sane human being, if they stopped to think for a moment, would espouse.

'Materialism' used in this sloppy sense to refer to an impoverished view about values must be clearly distinguished from a different use of the word, one which needs to be taken more seriously and raises some important philosophical questions. I have talked in the previous chapter about commitment to scientific knowledge as our best bet for understanding why the universe is as it is and why things happen as they do. Does that mean that the sciences are also our best bet for understanding ourselves, for understanding what human beings are and how they function? If so, this too may seem to carry the threat of diminishing us. It may seem to imply that human beings are nothing more than physical systems, like everything else in the universe, and can be understood in the same terms as any other physical system. That threat seems to increase with every advance in the biological sciences. Neurophysiology appears to have the potential to explain all our thoughts and feelings and hence all our actions in terms of electrochemical processes in the brain and the rest of the central nervous system. Modern genetics seems to hold out the prospect of explaining not only our physical characteristics but also our character traits and behavioural dispositions in terms of the particular constitution of the DNA we have inherited from our parents. So it looks as though it ought to be possible to explain how any individual human being is going to behave, in the same way that the engineer can explain the behaviour of a bridge or an aircraft, in terms of the materials it is made of and the way they are put together and the forces acting on them. This then is the other sense we can give to the word 'materialism', or what we might also call 'physicalism'. There is a good deal of disagreement about how to define these terms, and perhaps distinguish between them, with philosophical precision, but for our purposes let us say that materialism is the view that human beings are (just) physical systems.

The dilemma for atheistic humanism can then be put like this. On the one hand the word 'humanism' suggests a recognition of something importantly special and distinctive about human beings. On the other hand, because of its championing of scientific knowledge, humanism seems to be committed to a materialistic conception of human beings as physical systems and therefore as not radically different from anything else in the universe. This was a tension which we encountered in the first chapter. Modern atheists have adopted the term 'humanism' partly for the sake of a continuity with earlier connotations of the word, such as those of Renaissance humanism, celebrating the finer qualities of human beings and finding in them some kind of inspiration for a worthwhile life. But can atheistic humanism continue to draw on those associations while also allying itself with science to criticise religious beliefs?

What exactly is it that the materialist picture appears to be in danger of leaving out? What is it that we tend to think of as special and distinctive about human beings, and which seems to be threatened by this picture? Let us set aside religious conceptions and religious language for now, so as not to beg any questions, and let us try to answer the question in the neutral language of everyday experience. Well, we might say, the scientific materialist picture seems to leave out the *mental*. By that I mean not just our intellectual capacities, but our mental life construed more broadly, our thoughts, beliefs, emotions, feelings, experiences, sensations, hopes, fears, wishes, desires, choices and decisions. What we also think of as important is not just that we have these mental states and experiences but that they are *conscious* experiences. The possession of *consciousness*, we might say, is what makes us distinctively human.

CONSCIOUSNESS

'Consciousness' is another rather slippery term. In its more limited sense it just means 'awareness'. To be conscious of something in my environment is simply to be aware of it. If I swerve my car to avoid a hole in the road, then the hole, we might say, must have impinged on my consciousness. However, we tend more especially to use the word 'consciousness' to refer to something more than that, to our awareness of our own mental states and experiences. So though I was in some sense conscious of the hole in the road, we might say that I did not 'consciously' swerve to avoid it. Thinking about it afterwards, I might realise that that is what I had done, but perhaps at the time I was not conscious that I had seen the hole, that I had recognised that it was dangerous, that I had wanted to avoid it, and that I had realised that I needed to swerve in order to do so. Sometimes, then, we are not fully conscious of our own mental states, but in contrast we are for much of the time in our waking lives conscious of our own experiences and thoughts and feelings, and the richness of our mental lives depends crucially on our possession of consciousness in this strong sense.

One reason why consciousness is important is that it is a precondition of our capacity to *appraise* our own mental states, that is, our ability to stand back from them and think about them and evaluate them. We need to do this, for instance, in order to make rational decisions about our future actions, by reviewing our various, perhaps conflicting, desires, considering the reasons for and against acting on them and assessing the weight of those different reasons. We need consciousness in order to have hopes and aspirations for the future, which involves being able to anticipate our future feelings and desires, to think about their relationship to our present state, and to decide which ones are more important than others. We need consciousness in order to *evaluate* our actions, to think about what we have done and why we have done it, whether we should feel pleased or sorry at having done it, whether we should feel pride or shame. So consciousness is a precondition for our status as *moral* beings.

Closely linked with this is our possession of *freedom* or *free will*. We like to think that we can make our own free choices about what to do, and that though we cannot entirely control what happens to us, we can at any rate normally control our own actions and to that extent be the authors of our own lives. We resent attempts by others to coerce or constrain us because they threaten to rob us of that freedom. It is because we are conscious beings who can stand back from our experiences, can envisage alternatives to our present situation, can weigh up the alternatives and assess them in the light of our reasons for preferring one state of affairs to another, that we are not just prisoners of our immediate environment but can choose our actions and thereby make them our own. We saw in the first chapter that such very different humanists as Pico della Mirandola and Jean-Paul Sartre have concurred in identifying the capacity for free choice as a defining feature of what it is to be human. For Sartre, in particular, our possession of consciousness is what makes human actions free actions.

Consciousness is also a precondition of, but is not the same as, *self-consciousness*. By the latter I mean not just an awareness of one's own mental states and experiences, but an awareness of oneself as the continuing subject of those experiences. One might have consciousness but lack full self-consciousness. A very young child, for instance, might be aware of her own thoughts and feelings in the sense of being able to say what they are, but not yet have a clear sense of her identity as one person among others, as someone who once did not exist, who was born at a certain time and will die at some time in the future and will cease to exist, though the world will go on without her. Our possession of self-consciousness has important moral implications, as we shall see in the next chapter, and it builds on and extends further our possession of consciousness.

Consciousness, I have been suggesting, is something distinctively human. Non-living things like the bridge and the aircraft do not have it, and that is why we feel threatened if the scientific view of the world seems to treat us as physical systems on a par with them. Plants do not have consciousness, and I doubt whether other animals have it, or have it to any great degree. I do not want to make dogmatic claims here. The only non-human animals I have known well have been cats. I was unsentimentally fond of them and that fondness involved attributing various kinds of mental states to them. It would have been perverse not to allow such descriptions as 'He wants to be stroked', 'She is afraid of the noise', 'He thinks the piece of paper I'm pulling along is a mouse'. On the other hand I have no reason to suppose that they ever planned what to do the next day, that they ever felt pride or shame, or that they ever deliberated about whether it would be right to eat one another's food.

Other animal species may be more sophisticated than cats. I do not know much about chimpanzees or dolphins, for whom large claims are made, and it may be that they possess something closer to human consciousness, but if they do, I suspect that it is still fairly limited. It is difficult to see how a being could stand back from and appraise its own mental states unless it had a moderately complex language with which to identify and form beliefs about those states. So although I am not committed to any strong and dogmatic claim about the uniqueness of humans, I do think that there is a point in saying that consciousness is a special and distinctive feature of human beings, and I hope that what I have been saying brings out what is important about it.

This is the dilemma then. The term 'humanism' appears to imply the recognition of something special and distinctive about human beings, and it seems plausible to suggest that this distinctive feature is our possession of consciousness. If, however, humanists are also committed to the acceptance of a scientific understanding of the world, does that commit them to 'materialism'? Should humanists, if they are to be consistently committed to the scientific view of the world, accept that they have to regard human beings, and everything else in the world, as just physical systems? Would they then have to drop this idea of a special human attribute which is 'consciousness'? And does that then leave the way open for critics of humanism to say that only a religious viewpoint can do justice to the 'higher' aspect of human life?

What are we to make of these questions? Well, a great deal has already been made of them. There is a vast philosophical literature, some of it highly technical, dealing with what are standardly called the mind–body problem and the problem of consciousness. I cannot possibly do justice to it here or go into any of the detail, but for our present purposes I do not need to. I merely want to make some very general points about what emerges from the debate, and in particular to say something about what kinds of answers stand some chance of being acceptable, and what kinds of answers stand no chance at all. That, I hope, will be enough for my defence of humanism.

THE MENTAL AND THE PHYSICAL

We are to consider briefly, then, the various philosophical accounts of the relation between the mental and the physical. The first point to make about the debate is this. Any proposed account is a non-starter unless it can do justice to the acknowledged facts of our experience. The plain fact is that we do have conscious mental experiences. Our confidence in that fact is far greater than our confidence in any philosophical theory could be. Consequently if a proposed philosophical theory of the relation between mind and body would commit us to denying the obvious facts of our experience, there must be something wrong with the theory. What is more, we can be confident that the way in which we are conscious of our own mental states is quite different from the way in which we might know about physiological processes in our own or other people's bodies. I do not have to investigate what electrochemical processes are going on in my central nervous system in order to be aware of the pain that I feel, or to know that I am feeling depressed, or to be in a position to tell you what I believe. Note that I am not saying that we can never be mistaken about our own mental states. I am not denying that some people have more self-insight than others. What I am saying is that the fact of consciousness itself is more certain than any theory can be.

Most philosophical theories of the mind–body relation recognise this. It is generally accepted that one of the tests of the adequacy of any such theory is whether it can sufficiently account for these facts of our experience, and that a theory which fails to do so must be defective. I say that this is generally accepted, but it is not universally accepted. There are some philosophers who think that, in pursuit of an adequate theory which does justice to the scientific facts of neurophysiology, we shall have to jettison our everyday ways of talking about our conscious experience. This is the kind of position sometimes called 'eliminative materialism'. Its proponents sometimes refer to our everyday ways of talking about our conscious experiences – our vocabulary of 'beliefs', 'desires', 'intentions', 'emotions' and 'perceptions' – as 'folk psychology'. Folk psychology, they say, is a theory, and it is now a discredited theory which should be replaced by that of neuroscience. Just as the traditional geocentric theories of the heavens, enshrined in our everyday talk of the sun 'rising' and 'setting', had to be abandoned when it was realised that the heliocentric theory of the planetary system was a more successful one, so likewise the theory of folk psychology, however deeply enshrined in our everyday language, has to be abandoned in favour of its more successful scientific competitor.

There is an obvious point to be made against the eliminativists, that in abandoning folk psychology they would be depriving themselves of the very language which they need in order to state and defend their theory. They would no longer be able to talk of beliefs and claims and assertions, of reasons and the evidence of experience. But this objection is merely a particular version of the deeper point on which I have been insisting, that the core facts of so-called 'folk psychology' are more securely grounded than any theory which might purport to replace them. Our everyday conscious experiences and our everyday ways of talking about them are not a theory, they are the data which any theory has to give an account of. Without them, there is nothing for a theory of mind to be a theory of.

It might be said that the data for which folk psychology and neuroscience offer rival explanations are the facts of human behaviour, and that neuroscience can predict and explain our behaviour better than folk psychology can. But what is 'behaviour'? It is more than just the physical movements of our bodies. Even such simple actions as shaking hands with someone, or waving goodbye, let alone the myriad complex patterns of behaviour in which we engage, are more than just movements of the hand; they are meaningful actions inseparable from certain kinds of intentions and the understanding of social conventions. So the language of folk psychology, of beliefs and emotions and desires, is essential for the description of our behaviour. Without it, there are no actions to be explained.

DUALISM

Eliminative materialism, then, is a non-starter as a theory of mind and body. There is another position, at the other end of the theoretical spectrum, which also seems to me to be a non-starter. It is a position which was given its classic formulation by the seventeenth-century French philosopher René Descartes, but it goes back to Plato in the fourth century BCE, and it is a position which at first appears to reflect quite accurately our everyday ways of talking about mind and body. Its starts from the incontrovertible fact of experience which eliminative materialists seem to deny, that we do indeed have conscious mental states and experiences, and that we are aware of them in a way quite different from the way in which we might observe physical things in our environment including physiological processes in our own or others' bodies. Dualism, with apparent plausibility, infers that mental states and physical states must be states of two quite distinct kinds of things, minds and bodies. By 'body' Descartes means not just human bodies or the bodies of living things but any physical or 'corporeal' thing, and he suggests that the distinguishing feature of a body is that it is an 'extended' thing, that is, that it occupies space and thus has size and shape. A mind, in contrast, is a 'thinking thing' and its distinguishing feature is consciousness. So we get a picture of two separate worlds composed of two kinds of stuff, and mental states and physical states are distinguished by being assigned to these separate worlds.[1] Descartes's philosophy was in part prompted by the rise of modern science, especially the mechanistic physics of Galileo, and the challenge which it seemed to pose to the traditional religious view of the world. The 'two worlds' picture provides a way of reconciling the two. Science gives us knowledge of the physical world, in which everything can be understood as mechanical processes consisting in the movements of matter in space, leaving the mental realm for the soul, which Descartes identifies with the mind and which he thinks can exist independently of any body. (Descartes also thinks that non-human animals, since they do not have consciousness, do not possess souls and are simply machines.)

What is wrong with this? It looks like a theoretical version of common sense, and if we are insisting on the reality of conscious mental experiences and of a distinct kind of awareness of them, doesn't this lead naturally to dualism? The problem arises when, having made this radical separation of the mind and the body, we try to give a coherent account of how they interact. That they do interact is something which the dualist can hardly deny. Consider any simple action, say eating a biscuit. Certain sensations, prompted by states of my body, lead me to decide that I want something to eat. My desire to eat, together with certain beliefs such as that there is a packet of biscuits in the cupboard, and certain perceptual experiences such as seeing the packet, lead me to perform certain physical actions such as taking the packet from the cupboard, taking a biscuit from the packet, and putting it into my mouth. So we seem to have to talk about physical events causing mental events, such as states of my body producing a desire for a biscuit, and light waves striking my retina and producing the experience of seeing the packet. And we also seem to have to talk about mental events leading to physical events, such as my decision to eat a biscuit producing, via my actions, a change in the location of the biscuit. What is wrong with that account, then?

Two things in particular are wrong with it. First, if mental processes and physical processes are two such distinct processes, belonging to two quite separate entities, a mind and a body, how *can* they interact? We know what it is for one physical event to produce another physical event, but what is it for a physical event to produce a mental event or vice versa? Let us fill out the supposed story in a bit more detail. The physical states which give rise to my desire for a biscuit, such as the level of sugar in my blood, or contractions of the stomach, lead to the desire by causing further physical processes in my central nervous system. But now, if we are to believe the dualist story, these are mysteriously transformed into something mental, my feeling of hunger and my wish for a biscuit. And if we are to believe Descartes's version of the story, these mental events are features of a mind which has no spatial extension. The events therefore cannot be said to occur at any place, and we cannot describe the interaction between the processes in the brain and the mental experience of hunger by talking about the relative locations of the two events, in the way in which we could talk about one physical body impacting on another to cause movement in it.

Trying to fill out the details brings us to the second thing that is wrong with the dualist story. It implies that there are *gaps* in the physical sequence. The processes in the brain must stop when they are transformed into mental processes of experiencing hunger and deciding to eat, and then start again when the mental events produce more brain processes and muscle movements. But that cannot be right. There is every reason to suppose that the sequence of physical processes is continuous and uninterrupted, with each physical event causing the next, from stomach contractions to brain processes to movements of the muscles and limbs. Though we may not be able to describe the complete sequence in detail, the current state of scientific knowledge in physiology and neurophysiology is sufficient to identify the kinds of physical processes taking place at each stage and to leave us confident that there are no gaps or causal leaps in the sequence.

Since the physical causal sequence is complete and unbroken, and since it is also a matter of incontrovertible experience that there are such things as feelings of hunger, perceptual experiences, desires and beliefs and intentions, the dualist might be tempted to say that there must be two series of events proceeding in tandem. At some point the sequence forks, as it were, into a series of events in the brain and a parallel series of events in the mind, and the two then somehow come together to produce the act of eating the biscuit. But that cannot be right either. There is again the problem of how, on a dualist account, the two series of events can converge. There is also the problem that the mental sequence of sensations and desires and decisions and the physical sequence of neural events are not two separate and independent sequences. We know that they are correlated, so that different mental acts and experiences will involve correspondingly different brain processes. A decision to eat a biscuit will go with a different series of neural processes from the one which accompanies a decision to drink a cup of coffee, for instance. So a dualism which has the body and the mind working separately and in parallel is no more satisfactory than a dualism which has the body and the mind taking turns and causally interacting with one another.

The upshot is that dualism, insofar as it assigns conscious experiences to a separate entity called 'the mind' which does not occupy physical space, won't do. Any theory which radically separates 'mind' and 'body' in this way is thereby debarred from giving any coherent account of how the two come together. Since we have insisted, against the eliminativists, that there *are* such things as conscious experiences, it follows that they must be accommodated within one world, the physical world in which embodied human beings interact with other physical entities. In other words, any viable theory will have to be some form of non-eliminative materialism. It will have to treat talk of mental states and talk of the corresponding physical states as, in some sense, different ways of describing the same set of phenomena. This is the terrain on which various highly subtle and sophisticated philosophical theories compete, and where we need not go into details. One candidate, or group of candidates, would be some form of *identity* theory, asserting that mental processes such as thoughts and feelings are *identical with* the corresponding physical processes in the brain. The kind of identity in question would have to be what is called a 'contingent identity', like the identity of lightning and an electrical discharge, or water and H_2O, or colour and wave lengths of light. We do not *mean* the same by 'lightning' and 'an electrical discharge in the sky', and we learn what lightning is before we know anything about the scientific explanation of it, but it turns out that what we experience as lightning can be shown by scientific investigation to be identical with an electrical discharge. The relation between mental states and neurophysiological processes in the central nervous system might be something like that. An alternative formulation might be something like what is called a 'double aspect' theory, which treats mental states and the corresponding physical processes as different aspects of the same phenomenon, or perhaps a 'property dualism' which treats them as different properties of the same thing. The various alternatives need not concern us here. We need only to insist on the two fundamental points. First, any viable theory will recognise consciousness, the having of conscious mental states, as an undeniable, important and distinctive feature of human beings. Second, it will do so without assigning them to a mysterious entity called 'the mind' existing in some ghostly realm separate from the physical world.

I have defended the status of consciousness as a distinctive feature of human beings, distinctive in the sense that most, perhaps all, other species of living things lack it, and distinctive also in the sense that the possession of consciousness seems to be an essential precondition for things that give our lives value and purpose. I have suggested that we can take this position without having to link it to an implausible mind–body dualism. In the rest of this chapter I want to look briefly at the implications of this position by contrasting it with two sets of views which are, in very different senses, non-humanist.

IMMORTALITY

I turn first to the contrast with certain religious beliefs, and here what I want to say can best be brought into focus by looking at the traditional religious doctrine of the immortality of the soul. The word 'soul' is one of the more slippery items of religious vocabulary, but if talk of the soul surviving the death of the body is to mean anything at all, it must presumably be understood in terms of a mind–body dualism. It must refer to the idea that I could continue to have conscious mental experiences after my body has ceased to function and has been destroyed. On the view that I have been espousing, this is not a totally incoherent idea. I have agreed that there is a distinction between the mental and the physical in the sense that one can be aware of one's own thoughts and feelings in a way that does not depend on a knowledge of the physiological processes going on in one's brain and the rest of one's body. We can therefore at least make sense of the idea that after one's physical death these conscious mental experiences might continue, and since they could include memories of one's present life prior to one's physical death, this would mean that one could continue to exist as a person without one's body. However, though the idea is not incoherent, two strictly limiting comments need to be added.

The first is that a continuing existence of this kind would be an extremely attenuated existence. Without a body one would no longer possess sense organs, and one would therefore receive no sensory input or new stimuli of any kind. Deprived of a body, one would also be deprived of the means of talking or writing or communicating with other conscious beings in any way. It might, in reply, be said that we could perhaps have other, non-physical means of receiving new stimuli and of communicating, but in fact we have no idea what they could consist in, and no positive reason for thinking that that might be the case. The upshot is that such a continuing existence would be an existence shut in on itself, condemned to the perpetual recycling of the same old memories and thoughts. It would, I suppose, be hell.

The second limiting comment to be made is that, though the idea of such a continuing existence is not incoherent, all the evidence suggests that it is not in fact possible. I have argued that dualism is not plausible, and all the scientific evidence suggests that our mental experiences are dependent on physical processes in the central nervous system. I have acknowledged that precisely how that dependence should be formulated is a matter for philosophical dispute, but the dependence is real enough, and the least contentious way of putting it is that talk of our conscious thoughts and feelings is one way of describing what, at another level, turn out to be physiological and neurophysiological events in our bodies. We have every reason to believe, therefore, that when our brains and other bodily organs cease to function, our mental experiences will also cease.

To show that some kind of survival after death is a real possibility, and that it could be, if not heaven, at any rate something more attractive than the hell of mental isolation, one would have to give reasons for thinking that we may survive in embodied form. Two versions of this idea are offered by two different religious traditions. One is the idea of reincarnation, the idea that after my physical death and the destruction of my present body I might continue to exist, or be 'reborn', in another human body. Now the key question is what reason we might have for saying that this future embodied person is *me*. The only plausible answer is that there would have to be a continuity of consciousness from the one life to the other, and that means in particular that this future person would have to have memories of my present life in order to be me.

There have in fact been cases of people, often children, claiming to remember events and experiences from a 'past life'. In some cases these claimed memories have been shown to correspond to events and experiences which really did occur in the life of a particular person, and it is sometimes difficult to explain how the second person could have known of the experiences of the first person unless the memories were genuine, in which case the two people would actually be the same person. Is this evidence for reincarnation?

For it to be so, we would first have to rule out fraud. We would have to show that the child who claims to remember the past life of someone he or she never knew has not been fed information by adults who knew the earlier person. If this and other kinds of fraud, or unconscious prompting, were excluded, we would indeed have a phenomenon which is difficult to explain. Whether reincarnation is the best explanation is another matter. Certainly we have to recognise that such unexplained phenomena are extremely rare, and are therefore no evidence at all for reincarnation as a regular occurrence which happens to us all. It is hard to make any sense of the idea that most of us will be reincarnated but will forget our present lives. Without the continuing memories there will be no 'me' to be reincarnated. There is no separate 'soul' or mental stuff which could somehow be transferred from one body to another. The continuing existence of a person can only *consist* in either the continuity of the same body, or continuity of consciousness including memories. If both are absent, then talk of the 'same' person surviving from one life to the next becomes meaningless.

The idea of reincarnation, then, cannot be a plausible general account of what happens to us after death. If the immortality of the soul and reincarnation are both ruled out, is there any other way in which we might survive after our physical death? The orthodox Christian answer is: 'the resurrection of the body'. According to this doctrine, our bodies will be reconstituted, either immediately after our individual deaths or all together at the Last Judgement, and in this reconstituted bodily form we will continue to live and to experience the joys of heaven (or perhaps the torments of hell). It is quite unclear how this reconstituting of our bodies is supposed to occur. If it is supposed to be the revivifying of our present bodies, we know that these mostly either are burnt to ashes or rot and decompose in the ground, so for anyone whose body has met this fate it is too late for resurrection in that sense. Some bodies are to some extent preserved, even for centuries, in favourable conditions, as we know from the finds of archaeologists, but then those bodies do not seem to have been resurrected either. There remains the possibility that we will somehow be supplied with 'replica' bodies to enable us to continue to exist in embodied form.

What are we to say to this? The one thing to be said for it is that it is not open to the same objections as the idea of disembodied survival. On the other hand there is absolutely no evidence of any kind to support the belief that the resurrection of the body will actually occur. The only reason given by Christians for supposing that it will take place is that God has promised us, in the Bible, that it will. In other words, it is a matter of appealing to 'revelation'. No explanation is provided for how, against all the scientific evidence, such a thing could happen. It is, say the orthodox, a 'mystery'. It is indeed.

THEORETICAL ANTI-HUMANISM

I turn now to some views of a very different kind, often referred to as 'anti-humanist'. These are views influenced by Nietzsche and Heidegger, and especially by French structuralist and post-structuralist twentieth-century writers, calling into question the concept of 'man' as a tool of intellectual enquiry. Here is a classic passage from the French theorist Michel Foucault:

> One thing is certain in any case: man is neither the oldest nor the most constant problem that has been posed for human knowledge. Taking a relatively short chronological sample within a restricted geographical area – European culture since the sixteenth century – one can be certain that man is a recent invention within it. . . . And one perhaps nearing its end.[2]

This kind of theoretical anti-humanism is typically expressed in highly obscure prose, and I cannot claim successfully to have penetrated the obscurity, but there are some themes within it which bear on the issues I have been discussing in this chapter. The 'humanism' which these writers attack is not the atheistic humanism which I have been defending, but it is not totally unrelated, and I shall briefly try to make some connections.[3]

One such theme is that the very idea of 'the human subject' is a myth, conferring an illusory unity on what is really just a bundle of drives, or a 'site' for the interplay of forces generated by social or psychological or linguistic structures.

Theoretical anti-humanists are fond of invoking theories such as those of psychoanalysis, structuralist Marxism, or structural linguistics to demonstrate that the idea of the human subject as a unitary self has no explanatory value, and indeed that there is no such entity. Nietzsche seems to be an important influence here. He attacked as mere assumptions the 'rash assertions' 'that it is I who think, that it has to be something at all which thinks, that thinking is an activity and operation on the part of an entity thought of as a cause, that an "I" exists'.[4]

The idea that the word 'I' refers to an irreducible unitary self is, he says, 'a falsification of the facts', an interpretation imposed on our experience 'in accordance with the habit of grammar' which leads us to suppose that corresponding to the subject-predicate sentence 'I think' there must be a metaphysical subject, the 'I', which does the thinking.[5]

Nietzsche's target sometimes seems to be the specific religious or Cartesian equation of the self with a non-physical 'soul' or mental substance. He compares the undermining of this idea to the scientific discrediting of the traditional concept of the atom as an indivisible and irreducible unit of matter.

> One must also first of all finish off that other and more fateful atomism, which Christianity has taught best and longest, the *soul atomism*. Let this expression be allowed to designate that belief which regards the soul as being something indestructible, eternal, indivisible, as a monad, as an *atomon*: *this* belief ought to be ejected from science![6]

But, as we have seen, you can reject the religious view of the soul as an immutable spiritual substance without having to reject the idea of the self as a unitary consciousness. Nietzsche seems to be echoing a famous passage from David Hume about the systematic elusiveness of the self. Hume says:

> There are some philosophers who imagine we are every
> moment intimately conscious of what we call our *self*. . . . For
> my part, when I enter most intimately into what I call *myself*, I
> always stumble on some particular perception or other, of heat
> or cold, light or shade, love or hatred, pain or pleasure. I can
> never catch *myself* at any time without a perception, and never
> can observe anything but the perception. When my perceptions
> are removed for any time, as by sound sleep, so long am I
> insensible of *myself*, and may truly be said not to exist.[7]

What we call the 'self', Hume concludes, is really 'nothing but a bundle or collection of different perceptions'. But there is an irony in Hume's way of putting it, for what is it that he looks into when he fails to discover the unitary self he is seeking? It is his perceptions that he examines. Granted, these 'perceptions' – these sensations and thoughts and feelings and emotions and desires – are many and various and often in conflict with one another, but what makes them perceptions which belong to one and the same person is the consciousness which that person has of them. I am aware that this leaf which previously looked green to me now looks golden in another light, or that this feeling of anger is in conflict with this desire to keep the peace, and it is my awareness of these conflicting thoughts and feelings that makes them mine. We cannot get away from the fact that each individual physically embodied human being is aware of his or her own thoughts and feelings and experiences in a special way which differentiates them from the thoughts and feelings and experiences of others, and this is what we mean by the 'self' as consciousness.

As for the relevance of psychoanalytic accounts of the unconscious, it is indeed true that they introduce a further

level of complexity into the picture. Nevertheless the significance of repressed unconscious thoughts and desires cannot
be captured without recourse to the idea of the 'self'. The
unconscious desires which I repress are my desires, they are
ones which I have repressed. Though the existence of such
desires may complicate a simple equation of the self with
consciousness, we also have to bear in mind that if I have
repressed certain thoughts and feelings, I must initially have
been conscious of them in order to identify them as thoughts
and feelings which threaten me, which I cannot cope with
and from which I need to escape. Indeed, I must in some
sense, at some level, remain conscious of them in order to
maintain the repression. This is a point which some
philosophers (such as Sartre) have made in criticism of the
idea of 'the unconscious'.[8] It is difficult to formulate a coherent account which does justice both to the phenomena of
unconscious motivation and to the fact of the unity of consciousness. Nevertheless an account which attempts to eliminate talk of a unitary self altogether, to posit autonomous
desires which just buzz around with a life of their own, is less
satisfactory than one which recognises conflicts of desires
within the self, and recognises that they are conflicts just because
they are the desires of a single self.

Scepticism about the self, then, is one identifiable strand in
theoretical anti-humanism, and one which can be answered.
Another strand is scepticism about human nature. I quoted
Foucault as saying that discourse about 'man' is 'a recent
invention'. I am not sure what he is referring to here, and as it
stands it is a puzzling claim. Discussion of human nature and
of what it is to be human goes back at least to the thinkers of
ancient Greece. What is true is that the concept of 'man'
acquires a particular prominence in the eighteenth century,

when works such as Hume's *A Treatise of Human Nature* and Helvetius's *De l'homme* employ the idea of human nature as the synthesising concept around which knowledge can be organised. An account of the sources and limits of human knowledge, and of the passions which drive all human action, rather than a grand metaphysical scheme reflecting the divine design, provides the overarching philosophical structure. This commits such authors to generalisations about a universal human nature, shared by all human beings, and the danger with such claims is the risk of over-generalising. Beliefs and values and emotions may be declared to be universally human when they are in reality confined to one particular culture or social class. Talk of 'human nature' can then mask a cultural imperialism which judges human beings by the standards of one particular section of humanity. The danger is that such universalising talk masks the historically specific experiences of oppression and marginalisation which depart from the assumed paradigm of human nature – the experience of colonised or post-colonial societies, of women, of ethnic minorities, of sexual minorities, and so on. At the extreme, it may legitimate the labelling of some groups of human beings as 'less than fully human' or even as 'sub-human'.

Here is a particularly clear example of this criticism of humanism, one which sets the tone for much of the anti-humanism of French intellectuals in particular over the past fifty years. Reviewing an exhibition of photographs with the title 'The Great Family of Man', the critic Roland Barthes wrote:

> We are at the outset directed to the ambiguous myth of the human 'community' which serves as an alibi to a large part of our humanism. . . . Any classic humanism postulates that in

scratching the history of men a little, the relativity of their institutions or the superficial diversity of their skins (but why not ask the parents of Emmet Till, the young Negro assassinated by the Whites what *they* think of *The Great Family of Man*?), one very quickly reaches the solid rock of a universal human nature. . . . Birth, death? Yes, these are facts of nature, universal facts. But if one removes History from them, there is nothing more to be said about them; any comment about them becomes purely tautological. The failure of photography seems to me to be flagrant in this connection: to reproduce death or birth tells us, literally, nothing. . . . True, children are *always* born: but in the whole mass of the human problem, what does the 'essence' of this process matter to us, compared to its modes which, as for them, are perfectly historical? Whether or not the child is born with ease or difficulty, whether or not his birth causes suffering to his mother, whether or not he is threatened by a high mortality rate, whether or not such and such a type of future is open to him: this is what your Exhibitions should be telling people, instead of an eternal lyricism of birth.[9]

There are obvious truths in this passage, but they are half-truths. Of course the shared universal features of the human condition should not obscure the highly specific facts of inequality, of privilege and exploitation. But if there were no human nature, there would be no standpoint from which to identify these inequalities and injustices and to understand why they matter. If human beings were infinitely malleable, if there were no fixed human biological and psychological needs, it would make no sense to condemn as humiliating and degrading the living and working conditions which have been the lot of vast numbers of human beings, conditions which damage the body and stultify the mind and prevent people from fulfilling their human potential.

As a matter of fact, whatever progress there has been towards greater equality and the combating of injustice has been made possible by the clearer perception of what human beings share in common. The protest of oppressed groups has been that 'we are human beings like you', and progress comes when that truth is recognised – that other cultures are not 'barbarians' and 'savages', that their customs and practices are alternative ways of negotiating the same inescapable facts of the human condition, and as such may be as successful as, or superior to, those of the colonisers; or again, that the myth of women as creatures of 'intuition' rather than 'intellect' has served for millennia to prevent women from developing and using to the full their shared human powers of intelligence.

Given the naturalistic basis of human behaviour, and the fact that all human beings share a common genetic structure, it would be highly surprising if there were not universal human behavioural traits as well as universal biological features. It may be helpful to think of what is shared as a repertoire of potentialities which can be shaped in different ways in different cultures, rather than as fixed patterns of action and motivation. Sexual desire and sexual love are human universals, but the ideology of romantic love as the basis for monogamous marriage, for instance, is just one specific way in which a historically specific culture has shaped them. Human beings in all cultures laugh and smile, but what amuses them is notoriously variable and the sense of humour of one individual or culture can be very different from that of another. Fear and anger are universal human emotions; in some individuals and some cultures they come to the fore and manifest themselves in a preoccupation with power and domination and revenge, in others they are challenged and controlled in more benign ways. In these cases and others, there is no denying the facts of individual and historical and cultural specificity, but underlying them there is always the possibility of shared understanding. That possibility is rooted in a shared human nature, and in the next chapter we shall see why it is important.

I do not claim to have done justice to the complexities of theoretical anti-humanism, not least because I do not claim fully to understand them, and much of what it calls 'humanism' is not germane to our present enquiry. For our purposes it is enough that the idea of the human subject, defined by a unitary consciousness, and the idea of a shared human nature, can be defended.

ARE WE SPECIAL?

What then is special about being human? I have defended the view that there are certain distinctive features of human beings which are a precondition for the things we value. 'Distinctive' does not mean 'superior'. There is no standpoint from which we can compare ourselves with other species and declare ourselves to be a 'higher' species, the pinnacle of creation. The only possible such standpoint would be a god's-eye view, and Christianity has claimed to have access to it and to know that human beings were created 'in the image of God' to be the lords of creation.

> And God said, Let us make man in our image, after our likeness: and let them have dominion over the fish of the sea, and over the fowl of the air, and over the cattle, and over all the earth, and over every creeping thing that creepeth upon the earth.[10]

The growth of scientific understanding has dethroned the human species from this lordly position and destroyed this flattering picture. The universe does not exist for our benefit. We occupy a tiny portion of a universe which is immense in space and time. A recognition of our insignificance in relation to the rest of the universe is properly humbling, but it need not render our existence pointless, and it does not require us to deny what we take to be important features of our nature. Consider the following passage from a recent book by John Gray.

> Most people today think that they belong to a species that can be master of its destiny. This is faith, not science. . . . Darwin showed that humans are like other animals, humanists claim that they are not. Humanists insist that by using our knowledge we can control our environment and flourish as never before. . . . In the world shown us by Darwin, there is nothing that can be called progress. To anyone reared on humanist hopes this is intolerable. As a result, Darwin's teaching has been stood on its head, and Christianity's cardinal error – that human beings are different from all other animals – has been given a new lease on life.[11]

This is a classic example of a false antithesis, false because it deals in rhetorical abstractions. Gray thinks that we must choose between the belief that humanity is the master of its destiny and the belief that human beings are no different from other animals. The former belief would of course be absurdly pretentious. As Gray says, 'The idea of humanity taking charge of its destiny makes sense only if we ascribe consciousness and purpose to the species.'[12] 'Humanity' is not a conscious agent, the only conscious agents are human beings, and, as Gray revels in telling us, human beings have all too often made a mess of things, polluting the planet and inventing new forms of technology which solve some problems only to create new ones. But if we reject the absurd belief in the inevitability of the progress of humankind, it does not follow that we have to accept the equally absurd belief that human beings are no different from other animals. What is this supposed to mean? Which other animals? Gray's way of putting it implies that all animal species are alike, but that is nonsense. An amoeba is different from an elephant, a woodlouse is different from a chimpanzee, and if that is patently true, it is also patently true that humans differ from other animal species. We do not differ by being 'masters of our destiny', but we do differ by possessing the capacity to think about our situation, to assess what is good and bad about it, to weigh up different courses of action and try to change things for the better. Gray assures us that we are always bound to fail. Here is another of his false antitheses.

> The upshot of scientific enquiry is that humans cannot be other than irrational. . . . Humanists . . . do not deny that history is a catalogue of unreason, but their remedy is simple: humankind must – and will – be reasonable.[13]

The claim that human beings are always irrational is another of his rhetorical abstractions. Ironically, in the same paragraph he criticises humanists because 'their faith is just as irrational' as that of the theologians. In other words he castigates them for their irrationality and implies that they ought to be more rational. In so doing he subscribes, despite himself, to the simple and unexciting truths that we human beings sometimes behave rationally and sometimes behave irrationally, that we are therefore at least capable of rational thought and action, and that it is better that we should try to act and think rationally rather than irrationally. We can do this because, as humans, we possess those distinctive character-istics which are our capacities for consciousness of our own mental states, for assessing them and making choices in the light of our evaluations.

Four

In a much-quoted sentence from Dostoevsky's novel *The Brothers Karamazov*, one of the characters says, 'If God does not exist, then everything is permitted', and that is many people's fear – that if there is no God to underpin moral values, if values are simply human creations, then they lose their seriousness and 'it doesn't really matter what you do'. The assumption that morality collapses without a basis in religious belief is remarkably resilient and widespread. There are two intertwined claims here. There is the *factual* belief that if people do not see moral rules as emanating from the commands of a deity, they will as a matter of fact cease to have any concern for right or wrong. The second, deeper, claim is that if people respond in that way their response is rational, because if moral values are not backed by divine commands there is *no good reason* to try to live a morally good life. The second is the deeper claim because it asserts something about the very nature of moral values: they *are* essentially the requirements imposed on us by our divine maker, and, it is suggested, if we try to maintain values detached from that context they become groundless and we are engaged in an incoherent enterprise. The weaker claim is that, though in theory values can be divorced from any idea of divine commands, in practice most people will not be consistently and reliably motivated to act morally unless they think of moral requirements (whether correctly or mistakenly) as backed by a divine authority.

There is no denying that, historically, morality and religion have tended to go hand in hand. Most human beings in most human cultures have thought of rules for right living as rules imposed by a god or gods, and have thought of morally wrong actions as disobedience against divine authority. It is still the case, even in our own society, that if the press or other media are looking for a statement on some matter of moral significance, they tend to turn first to members of the clergy (and to a bishop if it is a really important matter). Is there a necessary link between morality and religion, then, or is the connection merely a historical one? I shall tackle the question by criticising the stronger of the two claims – that moral values *are* divine commands. In coming to see what is wrong with that picture I think we shall also see why it is that human beings *can* act well and live good lives without having to be motivated by a belief in a divine authority.

DIVINE COMMANDS

What is wrong with the view of morality as a set of divine commands? There is first the problem of how to identify what these supposed commands are. People hear voices telling them to do all kinds of things, some of them admirable, some of them terrible. Peter Sutcliffe, who in 1981 was found guilty of killing thirteen women and was dubbed by the press 'the Yorkshire Ripper', said that he had heard the voice of God telling him to kill prostitutes. The problem here is the one which we looked at in Chapter 2, of how to distinguish what is claimed to be a divine revelation from a delusion, a figment of the imagination or the product of a disturbed psychological state. More reliable, perhaps, than a claim to individual revelation might be a sacred book, hallowed by tradition and revered through the ages as the word of God. We again have the problem, however, that there are various texts with competing claims to that title. We also have the problem of how to interpret supposed commands in any such text. How do we distinguish deep moral truths from the historically arbitrary rules of a particular society? Is the famous verse in *Leviticus* which condemns homosexuality, and which biblical literalists take very seriously, really a direct moral command from God or just a feature of the strict code of a primitive desert people? (It is immediately preceded by the command not to have sex with a woman in her menstrual period, and closely followed by commands not to eat meat rare, not to have a 'short back and sides' haircut, and not to shave the edge of your beard.)[1] It is easy to mock, but consider a serious classic case. The 'Ten Commandments' in *Exodus* chapter 20 have been regarded as fundamental moral rules in Judaism and Christianity. They include the injunction not to kill. Many brave people have taken this literally, have refused to do military service, and have been imprisoned or even executed for their beliefs. Others have said that it should not be read as prohibiting all killing, only *unlawful* killing, and that it leaves room for the morally permissible taking of human life, for instance in self-defence. The important point here is that one cannot settle the question of interpretation without engaging in *independent moral debate*. The problem of how to interpret the command not to kill has to be resolved not by appealing to further supposed divine commands but by appealing to independent moral standards which do not themselves have any particular connection with religious belief. When we get into the debate about whether killing in self-defence is a legitimate exception, we are engaging in a moral debate which anyone, of any religious faith or none, can engage in. The same goes for the interpretation of any supposed divine command. To know what it means and what it should imply in practice, we have to invoke a shared moral understanding which logically *precedes* any particular religious beliefs.

This brings us to the more fundamental objection to the 'divine commands' picture of morality. It gets things the wrong way round. If there is a god, and if he or she commands or prohibits certain kinds of actions, that is because those actions are *independently* right and wrong. That is why they are commanded and prohibited. Killing is wrong because of the kind of action it is – the taking of a human life. It is the value of life that *makes* killing wrong. It is not that killing is wrong *because God forbids* it. It is that God forbids it (if he does) *because it is wrong*.[2]

The same point can be put in terms of the nature of moral motivation. People who perform or refrain from certain kinds of actions simply because they believe that this is what God commands them to do are not acting for genuinely moral reasons. What might their reasons be? They might be acting out of fear, aiming to avoid divine wrath and punishment either in this life or in a life to come. As supposedly moral motivation this is no better than the behaviour of the young child who obeys her parents simply because she does not want to be smacked, wants to avoid their anger, or wants to be given a sweet. Slightly more reputable might be acting in a certain way out of *awe* induced by a sense of the wisdom and power of a divine creator; but this is really no better than the behaviour of someone who blindly follows a teacher or a leader because they are mesmerised by that person's charisma. These kinds of motivation all look in the wrong direction, away from the action itself. In contrast, the genuinely moral reason, for example, for refraining from killing would be an understanding of the wrong that would be done to the *person killed*, together with a recognition of the devastating grief that would be caused for the bereaved. Likewise someone who is honest for genuinely moral reasons is someone who recognises what it is to deceive another person and recognises that this is no way to treat people. Someone who gives help and support to others for genuinely moral reasons is someone who is sensitive to people's needs and is moved by their needs and their suffering. And so on.

SUBJECTIVISM AND RELATIVISM

A proper understanding of what is mistaken about the 'divine commands' view of morality, and of moral motivation, points us towards the humanist alternative. As a first, over-simple, formulation of the contrast, we might say: moral values are not divine commands, they are *human* values. They are values which matter to us as human beings because of the kind of being we are, and because of the way in which we relate to our fellow human beings. That is essentially right, I think, but it is also liable to misunderstanding and needs to be clarified. There is a philosophical position, or more accurately a set of philosophical positions, which can be loosely referred to by the label 'moral subjectivism'. Essentially this is the idea that 'values' are to be distinguished from facts about the world. Values are not objective features of reality, existing 'out there', independent of us. When we say that something is right or wrong, good or bad, we are not making factual statements which can be true or false. We are expressing our feelings, emotions or attitudes towards the world, our own likes and dislikes, our feelings of approval or disapproval. That

is a simple version of the position, and it is one way of understanding the suggestion that values are 'human creations'.
Philosophical elaborations of it can be more complex and
subtle, adding refinements to deal with objections, and in the
end some sophisticated version of moral subjectivism might
turn out to be the best philosophical account of morality
(though I do not myself think so). I shall come back to it
shortly, but for the moment I want to distinguish sophisticated philosophical subjectivism from what I will call a
'crude subjectivism' which is all too common. This is the idea
that matters of right and wrong are 'up to you', that they are
'just your opinion' and that no one is in any position to
criticise anyone else or tell anyone else what they ought to do.
That is a view which many people unthinkingly hold, and
which many religious believers see as the unpalatable implication of the rejection of any divine basis for moral values. I
want to distinguish the humanist position from crude subjectivism. That is not what we are committed to if we assert
that moral values are, in some important sense, *human* values.

Closely akin to crude subjectivism is another popular view
which we can call 'crude relativism'. This is the idea that
values are simply the expression of the prevailing assumptions and conventions of a particular social group. It is often
backed up by the claim that 'we're all socially conditioned',
with the implication that different societies and cultures will
'condition' their members to adhere to different values. This
in turn is taken to imply that you can never criticise other
people's values or behaviour, because 'that's just your point of
view' and others are as entitled to 'their point of view' as you
are to yours. Just as this 'crude relativism' is indeed a view
taken by many people, so again the accusation of 'relativism'
is commonly made by those who want to insist on the

inseparability of morality and religion. As we shall see later, the accusation is confused and tends to run together different views under the label of 'relativism'. Like subjectivism, relativism is a position capable of being refined in philosophically subtle ways to make it plausible. What I want to insist on here is that a humanist position does not lead to 'crude relativism' as I have defined it, any more than it leads to 'crude subjectivism'.

SHARED HUMAN VALUES

Humanists will first want to emphasise that, if moral values are *human* values, that does not mean that they are arbitrarily dreamt up by individual human beings to reflect their individual likes and dislikes. They are *shared* human values. In the previous chapter I defended the idea of a shared human nature. For all the dangers of over-generalising, of extrapolating from the attitudes and assumptions of a particular culture or a particular epoch and falsely supposing that these are the attitudes and assumptions of all human beings, the fact remains that human beings are a biological species and that their shared biological nature brings with it a whole range of shared behavioural traits and shared needs. Most importantly for our present purposes, human beings are by nature *social* beings. Among animal species, and even among those which reproduce by sexual mating and must therefore be 'social' to at least some minimal extent, there are great differences in the degree to which they lead social or solitary lives. Human beings are the most social of creatures, for not only does their survival depend on social cooperation, but they engage in the most complex forms of cooperative activity. Foremost among these is the use of *language*, which in its turn makes possible all the myriad forms of social institutions – economic and political institutions together with the innumerable informal social groups formed around shared pursuits or intellectual and cultural endeavours or emotional ties. Our human capacity to understand a shared language both depends on and in turn promotes our capacity for emotional *identification* with one another – the fact that we are moved by one another's emotions, by one another's joys and sufferings. We have the capacity to imagine ourselves in other people's position and to feel what it is like to experience what they are experiencing. Not only *can* we, but we have some *propensity* to do so, in the sense that, other things being equal, the awareness that someone else is doing well is something pleasing and the awareness that someone else is suffering is upsetting. That is not to say that all human beings feel this (there are psychopaths and other human beings whose mental functions are severely impaired), and it is not to say that anyone feels this way all the time. Nevertheless it is a *characteristic* feature of human beings that we are inclined to relate to one another in this way, to the extent of sharing an impersonal value-language in which states of human happiness and flourishing are identified as good states of affairs and states of suffering and misery are identified as bad states of affairs, irrespective of who is experiencing them. In short, we *matter* to one another. It is this feature of human nature which the philosopher David Hume referred to as 'sympathy', as 'humanity' or 'fellow-feeling', and which he rightly identified as the precondition for shared moral values.[3]

It is important to be clear about how far this does and does not take us. I have said that our shared human capacity for imaginative emotional identification with one another is the *precondition* for shared moral values. That, of course, is no guarantee that we will always be motivated by, and act upon, a practical concern for one another. It does not solve the practical problems of human selfishness and partiality. What it does is to clarify the nature of such problems and put them in the right perspective. It explains how it is that these are problems which arise for us *as moral beings*. It is precisely because, as human beings, we think in moral terms, from the standpoint of moral values, that we can be exercised by our own and other people's failure to live up to those values, by our propensity to be tempted and distracted by selfish interests and partial concerns. This understanding of how our nature as social beings, and as beings who share a language, makes us also moral beings was given its classic formulation by Aristotle.

> It is clear why a human being is a social animal, more than any bee or any other gregarious animal. For nature, as we say, does nothing without a purpose, and humans are the only animals which have speech. Voice can be a sign of pain and pleasure, and so it belongs to the other animals, for their nature has developed to the point of having sensations of pain and pleasure and giving signs of them to one another, but speech is for indicating what is good and bad and so also what is just and unjust. For this is what is special to humans in comparison with other animals, that they have awareness of good and bad and just and unjust and so on, and it is sharing in these that makes a household and a city.[4]

Let us now return to the consideration of what I called 'crude subjectivism' and 'crude relativism'. I have been trying to bring out the difference between these positions and the idea of shared human values. The latter opens up the space for rational moral debate, appealing to shared standards and using reason and argument to try to arrive at the right answers to difficult moral problems. It does not cut short the argument, it does not prematurely leave disagreements unresolved and entrenched with the comment that 'that's just your point of view' and that 'we're all entitled to our own opinions'. Where, then, does this leave the philosophical debate between subjectivism and objectivism? Are our values in the end, as the subjectivists would maintain, the expression or projection of our own feelings and attitudes? Or are they, as the objectivists would maintain, independently existing features of the world, such that we can say that certain actions or states of affairs really are right or wrong, good or bad, regardless of what anyone happens to think about them? On the one hand, my defence of the idea of shared human values clearly makes them dependent on certain features of our nature as human beings. If it were not the case that as human beings we tend to identify with one another's feelings of pain and pleasure, joy and suffering in the way that we do, then we would not share the values which we do share. On the other hand, those values are standards which can be appealed to independently of what any particular individual or group happens to feel about this or that particular case. If an action is 'dishonest' or 'unfair' or 'cruel', or if it is 'kind' or 'considerate', those are objectively 'wrong-making' or 'right-making' features of the action, regardless of the particular responses of particular individuals or groups. To that extent there is something to be said on each side of the debate between 'subjectivism' and 'objectivism', and no simple answer to it.

Some philosophers have compared our recognition of values to our awareness of the so-called 'secondary qualities' of things – qualities such as colours and tastes and smells.[5] That we see things as red or blue, that things taste sweet or sour, that they smell fragrant or pungent, is in one sense dependent on the kinds of beings we are. For a species with quite different sensory apparatus, whose senses were not affected by things in the way that ours are, things would not be red or sweet or whatever. On the other hand, something's being red or sweet or fragrant is independent of how any particular human being or group of human beings happens to perceive it on any particular occasion. If, because of a trick of the light, we see this red rose as green, then we are mistaken, and in that sense it 'really is red'. What is more, the minority of human beings who are red/green colour-blind really *are* colour-blind. They are unable to discriminate between things which really are differently coloured. The analogy between values and secondary qualities has its limitations, but it is useful in bringing out how the existence of values, like the existence of colours and tastes and smells, both is and is not dependent on human responses. So does this make them subjective or objective? The same philosophical debate takes place with secondary qualities as it does with values, and for our present purposes we can take leave of the debate as it enters into further refinements over the precise meaning of 'subjective' and 'objective'. If values can be real in something like the way that colours and smells and tastes can be real, if it can be as true that something is right or wrong, just or dishonest, as it is that a rose is red or honey is sweet, that will be enough.

UTILITARIANISM

I have been talking in very general terms about 'shared human values'. It is time to be more specific. What are they? Here is one suggestion which looks appealing, and which some humanists have thought sufficiently appealing to be the last word. If our values are distinctively human values, it may be said, then the ultimate value is the value of human well-being, the achievement of human happiness and the prevention or elimination of human pain and suffering, and all our more specific values and actions should be judged by their tendency to promote happiness and prevent suffering. That is the moral theory commonly known as 'utilitarianism'. In its classic formulation by the nineteenth-century philosopher John Stuart Mill, it is the view that 'actions are right in proportion as they tend to promote happiness, wrong as they tend to promote the reverse of happiness'.[6] The happiness in question is not just one's own happiness but that of anyone affected by the actions in question. In short, the test of right and wrong is 'the general happiness'.

This theory has two attractions in particular. First, it appears plausibly to account for our more specific values. Why is it normally wrong to kill? Because it cuts short the happiness of the person who is killed, and causes terrible grief and suffering for the bereaved. Why are values such as honesty and fairness important? Because it is only if we can rely on one another, and deal fairly with one another, that we can cooperate effectively and reap the benefits of social cooperation. Why do we praise the qualities of kindness and consideration? Because these are the qualities which lead us to try to promote one another's happiness and relieve one another's suffering.

Secondly, the theory appears to offer a way of resolving difficult moral dilemmas. Sometimes different values conflict, and we have to make tough choices. Normally we value honesty, for instance, but sometimes the truth is difficult for people to bear, and it may seem kinder to withhold from someone, say, the seriousness of his medical condition, or the cutting things which other people are saying about her. What should we do? A plausible answer seems to be: work out what will do the most good in this particular case. And that means taking into account all the consequences, long-term and short-term, both for the person most directly affected and for others indirectly affected, weighing them up and doing what will produce the greatest overall long-term happiness or the least suffering.

Note also some other features of the utilitarian approach, and in particular the difference between it and a certain kind of religious morality. It is an approach which recognises that there is more to the moral life than a set of simple general rules. Such rules have their place – 'Do not kill', 'Do not inflict cruelty', 'Tell the truth', 'Keep your promises', and so on – but they are not 'absolutes', they cannot be followed unconditionally and without exception, since they sometimes conflict. In cases of conflict there is, according to the utilitarian, no alternative to a careful and detailed weighing up of the foreseeable consequences. In that sense, from a utilitarian point of view, what is right or wrong depends on the particular circumstances.

Note further that the utilitarian approach to morality is a very demanding one. Even in those areas of our lives where we *can* live in accordance with simple traditional moral rules, it is not *enough* simply to do so. There is more to the good life than simply avoiding the more spectacular kinds of wrongdoing. The utilitarian approach requires us to do *as much as we can* to promote the greatest happiness and to eliminate suffering. So even if we lead respectable lives, and do not actually kill or rape or cheat or steal, there is, for most of us, more that we could do in the way of positive good. There are innumerable opportunities for further acts of kindness and concern both towards those closely connected to us and for others more remote from us, and indeed for future generations yet to be born. There are the facts of poverty and disease, the sufferings created by war and exploitation and injustice on a global scale, which we can all make some contribution to alleviating.[7] So, to a certain kind of high-minded religious believer who claims that only religious faith can furnish a noble ideal to aspire to, the utilitarian can reply that religion has no monopoly on such inspiring ideals. The injunction to 'love your neighbour as yourself' is just one specific expression of the universal principle of aiming to do good in the world, to promote the well-being of one's fellow human beings.

The utilitarian approach is a good place to start. It does indeed have the plausibility which is assigned to it. It rightly asserts the possibility of a purely secular morality. It rightly emphasises the complexity of moral decision-making, the importance of attention to consequences, and the limitations of simple general rules. However, it is *not complex enough*. It draws attention to some important features of any humanist morality, but it leaves things out. It is too simple. And I suggest that looking for what it leaves out is a helpful way of arriving at a more satisfactory picture of what a humanist morality should be.

CARE AND RESPECT

Note first that utilitarianism focuses on one kind of moral concern for others. We are supposed to promote their happiness and prevent their suffering. Some would say that you cannot *make* someone happy. That is at best a half-truth. You cannot force people to feel good about their lives, but you can help them to do so. You can contribute to their material well-being in all sorts of ways, you can perform tasks for them which they may be unable to perform for themselves, you can look after them if they are sick, you can provide friendship and comfort and support, and certainly you can try to avoid the many kinds of nastiness whereby we inflict physical and mental pain on one another. Still, there is a half-truth here: you cannot take over someone's life and run it for them, you cannot decide for them what they are to make of it. We may be all too tempted to do so. Most obviously, those of us who have been parents are familiar with the desire to make our children happy, and consequently to make their decisions for them, to decide for them who their friends should be, what pursuits they should engage in, what choices they should make about their education and career and life-style. What we learn, however, is that you have to let go, that you have to let your children make their own mistakes, even at the cost of their happiness, because that is part of what it is for them to live their own lives. Now you might say that the lesson learned here is that, in order to be happy, people need to make their own decisions, and that the utilitarian approach can accommodate this within its advocacy of happiness as the ultimate value. I suggest that it may be more helpful, however, to distinguish between two kinds of concern for others. Utilitarianism focuses on the relationship between oneself as *agent* and the other as *recipient* of the benefits or harms one produces for them. As an exclusive focus, however, this fails to do justice to the fact that we have to relate to others also as *agents in their own right*, with their own lives to live. There are, we might say, two basic kinds of concern for others, that which takes the form of *care* and that which takes the form of *respect*. By 'care' I mean acting on others' behalf, with the aim of doing good to them and promoting their well-being. By 'respect' I mean recognising that they can and must also act on their own behalf, in the light of their own feelings and beliefs and aspirations. 'Respect' means respect for other people's sense of themselves, for their dignity, for their autonomy, for the space which they need in order to create meaningful lives for themselves. Both kinds of concern are important, and there is no easy way of balancing them against one another (as, again, we know all too well from our experience as parents and/or as children).

In distinguishing between the two kinds of concern, I have, so far, been warning against what we can call 'paternalism', the tendency to promote others' well-being on their behalf and thereby restrict their freedom to make their own decisions. I want now to suggest that the distinction points also towards another limitation of the utilitarian view. Utilitarianism is essentially an *aggregative* morality. It requires us to promote the general happiness, and that means doing *as much good as possible*, not just for particular others but for people in general (including, of course, the pursuit of one's own happiness as one among others). Now, inescapably, people's interests often conflict, and we have to make tough choices between them. The utilitarian solution is to *maximise* the good consequences – to do what will produce the greatest overall benefit. Undoubtedly we do sometimes think like this. Where are we to spend the family holiday this year? Maybe we cannot satisfy everyone. If Abbi would love a holiday at the seaside but Ben, Clare and Doug would hate it, whereas Ben, Clare and Doug would all enjoy a holiday in the country and Abbi wouldn't mind it, then the greatest overall enjoyment will be produced by going for the country option. The same approach is at work in a lot of public decision-making: the new bypass will make life better for a great many people; unfortunately it will also lower the quality of the lives of a few people who will now have traffic passing closer to their homes, but their interests have to be outweighed for the sake of the greater good. That is the aggregative approach, and in many cases it makes sense, but in some cases it can seem much more disturbing. It opens utilitarianism to the accusation that it could sometimes justify doing terrible things to some people for the sake of the greater good. Some standard counter-examples which have been used to criticise utilitarianism are that, for example, it could justify killing an innocent person to appease an angry mob, on the grounds that worse consequences overall would occur if this were not done. Or again, it is said that utilitarianism could in principle justify slavery provided the benefits to the slave-owners were so great as to outweigh the slaves' loss of well-being.

What utilitarianism fails to take on board, it seems, is that though some people's interests sometimes have to be sacrificed for the interests of others, there are limits. There are some things which, morally, you cannot do to people for the sake of the greater good. My distinction between two kinds of concern helps us to see why this is so. Human beings are not just recipients of well-being, experiencers of happiness. They are also separate and unique individuals, each with his or her own life to lead. They are not simply constituents of one great heap of well-being. Of course not everyone can get everything they want, and sacrifices have to be made, but if one person is sacrificed to the extent that they no longer have a life of their own, then we cannot simply see this as a loss to be compensated for by the production of greater good elsewhere. It is an absolute loss. So, for instance, if innocent people are unjustly killed, it is not enough to point out that more people will benefit overall. Nothing can compensate for the irreplaceable life which is lost. Likewise freedoms sometimes have to be restricted, but if people are entirely deprived of their free-dom, by being enslaved or unjustly incarcerated or in some other way, then they too are being deprived of the only life they have.

A classic philosophical formulation of this idea is the moral philosophy of the eighteenth-century philosopher Immanuel Kant. Kant says that we should treat human beings 'never solely as means to an end, but always also as ends in them-selves'.[8] This is not entirely perspicuous. We use people as means to an end, quite innocently, all the time – whenever we make use of the services of shop assistants and taxi drivers and train drivers, of teachers and doctors. Yes, Kant might say, that is acceptable as long as we do not treat them *only* as means but *also* as ends. But what does that mean? That it's OK as long as we pay them, or smile and say thank you? Does that mean that it is acceptable to make use of another human being as a slave provided that you treat them well and take a personal interest in them? Another formulation which Kant uses is the one which I have used above, that we owe human beings *respect*, and he links this with the idea of treating one another as *persons* rather than as mere *things*. This is still not very precise, but perhaps precision is not to be looked for. The contrast between 'persons' and 'things' at any rate has the advantage of bringing out the humanist credentials of these ideas. It draws on the position I defended in the previous chapter, that there is indeed something distinctive about being human, and that it has to do with our capacity for *conscious* experience. This brings with it the capacity to shape our own lives rather than just be shaped by the causal influences of our environment, the capacity to step back from our circumstances and to assess them and to respond to them in the light of our own projects and feelings and aspirations. It is in this way too that we can make sense of the idea of individual human lives as irreplaceable. Each human being is a unique centre of consciousness, a unique perspective on the world, a unique set of experiences and emotions and beliefs and concerns. So to sacrifice a human life for the sake of the greater good is, in that sense, to destroy something irreplaceable. And to deprive a person of their autonomy and their capacity to direct their own life, to ignore their own feelings, is to treat them as less than human, as a mere object.

The idea that there are moral limits to the permissible treatment of human beings, for however great a good, can also be articulated in the language of *human rights*. The use of the vocabulary of rights has escalated over recent decades. It is put to a variety of uses, perhaps all legitimate but certainly not always clearly distinguished. Rights are claimed and ascribed without any clear criterion for determining what rights there are and where the list ends. One significant use of the language of rights, however, is to set limits to utilitarian calculations.[9] So to talk of each individual's *right to life* is to recognise that human lives are not just items to be weighed against one another in a utilitarian calculation of total net benefit. If I have a right to life, that means that other people may not deprive me of that right; my life is *mine*, not just a component of the general happiness, and it is for me to decide what is to be done with it. Likewise the rights to certain basic freedoms establish the constraints on the ways in which human beings may be treated, and to violate those rights is to begin to rob them of their humanity.

I said that the use of the vocabulary of 'human rights' has grown. The first two great declarations of rights were the American *Declaration of Independence* (1776) and the French *Declaration of the Rights of Man and Citizen* (1789). The language of rights was given new prominence after the Second World War, as an appropriate way of expressing a world-wide determination to try to prevent a repetition of the horrors of Nazism and of total war. Two important documents to emerge were the *United Nations Universal Declaration of Human Rights* (1948) and the *European Convention on Human Rights* (1950), which was in 1998 incorporated into British law. One disconcerting feature of these various declarations is the discrepancy between the rights which are listed, ranging from the American Declaration's rights to 'life, liberty and the pursuit of happiness' to the more than thirty rights listed in the United Nations Declaration. This may encourage the thought that any such list is bound to be an arbitrary one, and this may in turn appear to support the criticism that the very idea of human rights is suspect – that it has no objective rational basis, and is a piece of 'cultural imperialism', an attempt to give spurious world-wide legitimacy to ideas which are the particular product of the western liberal tradition.

If we look more closely at the different lists, however, I think we can see a certain logic to the discrepancies. The European Convention, for instance, is essentially a list of negative rights – rights to be allowed to do certain things, and rights not to be treated in certain kinds of ways. They include the right to life, rights not to be tortured or enslaved, and rights to freedom of thought and freedom of expression. These are the kinds of rights to which I referred above, reflecting the idea of moral constraints on people's treatment of one another. The United Nations Declaration includes all these rights, but adds others, positive rights such as the right to social security, to equal pay, to rest and leisure, to education, and to a standard of living adequate for the health and well-being of oneself and one's family. These are 'positive' rights in the sense that they are goods which, it is implied, every society ought to be able to guarantee for its members. The two kinds of rights reflect the different kinds of human needs and interests which I have discussed in this section, and the two kinds of moral concern, that of respect and that of care. Both kinds of rights, therefore, are grounded in deep facts about human nature, in universally shared human needs to enjoy certain kinds of goods, to be free to act in certain kinds of ways, and to be protected from certain kinds of treatment. The charge of arbitrariness can therefore, I think, be met, and the growth of the language of human rights as an internationally shared moral vocabulary is something to be welcomed. The language of rights cannot do all the moral work, it is not a comprehensive moral vocabulary, but it is one way of articulating a core set of moral considerations.

The distinctions and contrasts which I have been making in this section are the matter of long-standing debates in moral philosophy, about the relative merits of Kantian and utilitarian moral theories, of rights-based and goal-based moralities. Whatever the conclusions of these debates may be, I think that looking at these ideas from a humanist perspective can help us to see that they reflect different aspects of what it is to be human. Human beings are affected by the actions of other people, they are the recipients of benefits and harms conveyed by others. Human beings are also conscious subjects who have their own emotions and beliefs, who make their own choices and shape their own lives, for good or ill. Hence we owe one another both kinds of concern, that which involves promoting the well-being of others, and that which involves respecting the autonomy of others and accepting that their lives are their own. Both are equally important acknowledgements of what it is to be human, and both are therefore equally important components of a humanist morality.

UNIVERSALISM AND SPECIAL RELATIONSHIPS

One of the impressive features of utilitarianism is its universalism. It enjoins a concern for *all* human beings. In aiming to promote the general happiness, we are to weigh equally the claims of all whose happiness we can affect. The same amount of happiness is equally valuable, whether it is felt by me, or by those who are like me and close to me, or by human beings whom I do not know, in other parts of the world, or by future generations not yet born. This looks impressive insofar as it is a rejection of the partialities of race and sex and class. If all human beings count equally, then to exclude some or to downgrade their interests because 'they're black' or 'women are inferior' is to be guilty of an irrational prejudice, the denial of a fully human status to those who happen to be different from oneself. This universalism is another feature that makes the utilitarian approach attractive to humanists. It makes the link between humanism and humanitarianism. That is not to claim that humanists have any monopoly on humanitarian concern, but simply to say that the recognition of a shared human nature, and a shared propensity of human beings to identify with one another's feelings and experiences, gives rise to a morality which acknowledges the needs and interests of all.

This admirable refusal to give special priority to the interests of one's own social group may come to seem less appealing, however, if it excludes certain other kinds of special ties and loyalties. What about our special attachments to friends and lovers, parents and children? Are these simply to be dissolved in an undiscriminating devotion to every fellow human being? Am I to refuse to do a good turn for a friend, or to make special provision for my children, on the grounds that the relationships I have to them should be no different from my obligations to all other human beings?

That would be absurd, and there are various responses available to the utilitarian. One would be to say that of course utilitarianism does not require us to divest ourselves of our special relationships and affections. It is not the job of the theory to tell us whom to love. The 'general happiness' principle is a *moral* principle, and it comes into play only when we are looking at our actions from a moral point of view.

To me that hardly seems to be satisfactory. How are we supposed to demarcate the jurisdictions of morality and of other perspectives such as that of personal relationships? Suppose that every day I visit a sick friend. Suppose that I then ask myself whether this use of my time is *morally* right and, mindful of the general happiness principle, I reflect that I could be devoting that same time to raising money for the alleviation of world hunger, or campaigning for the freedom of oppressed political dissidents, or doing voluntary work in the local hospice. Does my decision whether to visit my sick friend then become absorbed in the general calculation of which course of action will promote the greatest happiness? If not, how am I supposed to draw the line between the moral decision and the other kinds of practical decisions I have to make?

This idea of the moral point of view as a distinct perspective from which to think about how to live is one which we ought to question. I suspect that it is at least in part the product of a religious way of thinking. It is in part a legacy of the idea of moral rules as divine commands. The idea of a distinctive sense of wrong-doing which is moral guilt, the feeling of a guilty conscience, is partly explained as the residual idea of having offended against a divine law-giver, a divine judge before whom we are guilty. The understanding of 'morality' as a distinct perspective or institution is not to be found in the thought of the ancient philosophers. When Aristotle discusses what are standardly translated as 'the moral virtues', he is simply talking about the qualities of *character* (as distinct from the qualities of *intellect*) which are possessed by a good human being. Neither he nor Plato would understand the question of what 'morality' requires of us. For them the practical question is simply the question of what it is to live a good human life.

A secular humanist philosophy needs to recapture that way of thinking. Our obligations to our fellow human beings need to be seen not as the distinctive province of a 'peculiar institution' called 'morality' but as part of a whole way of life.[10] As social beings we are each of us embedded in a complex network of relationships. These include close personal ties, sustained by intense emotions or enduring affections. They include also our wider loyalties to colleagues and fellow-citizens. And as part of the same picture, they include responsibilities to all other human beings, sustained by our sensitivity to human needs and human suffering. Of course there will always be conflicts between the different demands which these different relationships make on us. If faced with the choice, do I betray my friend or my country? What do I do if my responsibilities at work, or the time I give to the support of a charity organisation, are making inroads on the time I spend with my family? But the way to think about resolving such conflicts, difficult though it may be, is not to appeal to some moral rule or to a principle of the greatest happiness, but to think about the place which each of these kinds of relationships and responsibilities has in a meaningful and fulfilling human life.

THE FULLY HUMAN LIFE

This notion of a fulfilling human life, and the reference to Plato and Aristotle, may prompt some thoughts about the preoccupation with happiness. I have been referring more or less interchangeably to the ideas of 'well-being' and 'happiness'. The classical utilitarians explicitly identified them, but to do so, and to commit humanism to that identity, may seem to incur a charge of superficiality. Has life, it may be asked, no nobler and higher goal than happiness? Aldous Huxley's famous dystopian novel *Brave New World* imagines a future society in which everyone is happy, because the system provides them with a ceaseless supply of trivial pleasures, in the form of electronic games, multi-media entertainments, casual sex and hallucinatory drugs. There is no suffering, no dissatisfaction or frustration, and none of the intensity of tragedy. There are no conflicts and no challenges, and no ideals to strive for. As Brave New World seems to come ever closer to reality, some would say that this reveals the shallowness of a humanist perspective which can identify no higher goal than merely human satisfactions, because it has no sense of the transcendent. Is the pursuit of happiness a recipe for triviality?

Well, it depends what you mean by 'happiness'. The Greek word 'eudaimonia' which Plato and Aristotle standardly employed to identify the goal of human life is most frequently translated into English as 'happiness', but that is not a perfect translation. Eudaimonia is not primarily a state of feeling, but a state of objective flourishing. Aristotle gives a distinctively humanist gloss to this. To know what eudaimonia is, to know what it is for a human being to flourish, we have to look at what makes us distinctively human. What marks us out from other species, he says, is our capacity for rational thought, and to flourish as a human being is therefore to exercise that capacity to the full, both in the use of rational judgement in practical affairs and in the theoretical contemplation of intellectual truths. The ideal of eudaimonia is the ideal of the fully human life.[11]

The nineteenth-century utilitarian John Stuart Mill takes up this idea and thinks that the meaning of the English word 'happiness' is sufficiently rich to accommodate it. Like Aristotle he thinks that in order to understand what happiness consists in for a human being we have to look at what it is that makes us human.

> Few human creatures would consent to be changed into any of the lower animals, for the promise of the fullest allowance of a beast's pleasures. . . . A being of higher faculties requires more to make him happy, is capable probably of more acute suffering, and certainly accessible to it at more points, than one of an inferior type; but in spite of these liabilities, he can never really wish to sink into what he feels to be a lower grade of existence.[12]

This leads Mill to introduce a distinction between 'higher pleasures' and 'lower pleasures', the former being the distinctively human 'pleasures of the intellect, of the feelings and imagination'.[13] Note by the way that it is not just the pleasures of the intellect. Mill is sometimes accused of being an intellectual élitist, but he ranks a rich emotional life and imaginatively creative activity as equally important. The important point is that Mill shares with Aristotle the authentically humanist ideal of the fully human life, not a life of superficial satisfactions but a life enriched by the striving to use all our human potentialities to the full. As he famously puts it, 'it is better to be a human being dissatisfied than a pig satisfied; better to be Socrates dissatisfied than a fool satisfied'. Once again we see the relevance, discussed in the previous chapter, of what is special about being human.

HUMANS AND OTHER ANIMALS

I have been talking of a humanist view of life as one guided by human values, and so far that has led me to focus on our concern for other human beings, and on what it is to lead a full and happy human life. This may seem to invite a familiar charge – that humanists are only interested in human beings, and are bound to neglect the claims of other animals and the rest of the living world. I need to respond briefly to that charge.

The reason for stressing what is distinctive about human beings, and the differences between them and other animals, is to make the point that what constitutes a good life for a human being is different from what constitutes a good life for a cat or a chicken. Still, the life of a cat or a chicken or any other animal can go well and it can go badly, and that matters. Non-human animals can experience pain and pleasure, they can suffer. Utilitarians have standardly insisted that if happiness and the absence of suffering are the sole ultimate values, then that must mean that we should aim to promote the well-being and prevent the suffering of *any* being capable of experiencing pain or pleasure – that is to say, of all sentient living things. We should not be misled by Mill's apparently disparaging remark about pigs: a human being cannot wish to live the life of a pig, but there is nothing wrong with a pig doing so. As humans we have obligations to other animals to enable them to live lives free of pain, if we can do so, and to avoid inflicting unnecessary suffering on them. In the modern world that means, especially, opposing farming practices which are cruel to animals, and opposing the use of animals for laboratory experiments which inflict needless pain on them.[14]

That is essentially right, I think. Humanists should not limit their concern to humans. At the same time I want to repeat my earlier qualification to the idea of promoting 'the general happiness'. That, as I argued, should not mean an abstract universalism. Our concern for all other human beings takes its place within a meaningful human life which is shaped also by our more particular relationships with particular people. The same goes for our concern for non-human animals. It is a truism, but an important one, that animals matter to us because they have a significance for us. That does not mean that we should regard animals as existing simply for our use. On the contrary, an important aspect of the place which other animals have in our lives is precisely that they are non-human. Humanists are sometimes accused of adopting a cosy, parochially human perspective which excludes the rest of nature. There is no reason why they should do so. Our encounters with the natural world are encounters with what is irreducibly *other*. Humans may tame the natural world and use it for their own purposes, but it is important also not to lose our sense of what is alien and distant in nature. It is what underpins our feelings of awe and reverence for the natural world. These feelings of its strangeness, of mystery when confronted with other living things, are reminders of the limits of our human perspective, and they help us to define what it is to be human. This goes for our relations not just with other animals, but also with inanimate nature. It is important for us that there should be wild places, barren landscapes, impenetrable mountain ranges and inhospitable deserts – not so that we can visit them and enjoy them, but, on the contrary, because they exclude us. In these ways, humanists can and should want to preserve the natural environment, as well as showing concern for the welfare of non-human animals – but that concern has a dimension which is properly *different* from our concern for other humans.

Having said that, I want to add that there are also immensely strong *instrumental* reasons for humanists to be concerned about the natural environment, reasons grounded in human interests including the interests of future generations. We do not want to live in a world where there is no pure air to breathe, no clean water to drink or to bathe in, where fields and woods are destroyed in order to build yet more motorways and airport runways, where agricultural land is overused and becomes infertile, where pesticides which protect agricultural crops also kill butterflies and skylarks. We want to prevent these things from happening, because they will all lower the quality of our lives, will deprive us and our successors of the enjoyment of beauty, and in the long term threaten human needs for food and good health. All these are overwhelmingly good reasons for humanist environmentalism, to be set alongside our sense of awe at the otherness of the natural world.

WHY BE GOOD?

At the beginning of this chapter I distinguished two kinds of scepticism about the possibility of morality without religion. I have answered the stronger version. I have argued that there are shared human values, grounded in our nature as human beings, which are entirely independent of religious belief. They constitute a rational basis for views of how we ought to live. The weaker form of scepticism, however, remains to be answered. It may be that though there is a rational secular humanist understanding of what constitutes a good human life, most people are incapable of living by it. It may be that most people will not live and act as they should without external sanctions, those of the law and punishment, but also the sanctions provided by belief in a divine being who commands us to live in the right way and will punish those who disobey. If that is the case, then perhaps we ought to encourage belief in a super-human law-giver, even though we know it to be an illusion. Perhaps human life will go badly if we don't.

Such a position would be an explicitly élitist one, but that is not yet a sufficient objection to it. Perhaps some people just do possess to a greater degree than others the psychological resources needed to live a good life. Unpalatable though it may be, might it not be the case that you and I, who think about these things and read books on humanism, belong to a relatively élite group, and should refrain from undermining the illusions of those who need them?

That could be true, but I do not think that it is. It is pretty clear that some people are cleverer than others, and no doubt you, the reader, are cleverer than most, but I hope you will agree that this does not make you morally superior. The qualities which are needed to live a good life are not primarily intellectual abilities, but practical intelligence, a balanced insight into the realities of particular situations and, as I have argued, a capacity for imaginative and sympathetic identification with the needs and experiences of others.

Still, it might be said, those are qualities which are hard to come by. Indeed, the pessimist will maintain that they are unattainable. Human beings, it may be said, are inherently selfish; the whole of human history bears witness to the fact that human beings will do terrible things in pursuit of their own blind and selfish interests, and there are biological imperatives which make this inevitable. Does not evolutionary theory tell us that only the fittest survive in the struggle for existence? Are we not all mere vehicles for 'the selfish gene'?

Let us take the evolutionary point first. The phrase 'the selfish gene' was coined by Richard Dawkins.[15] It is a metaphor, a striking one, but not one which supports the claim that human beings or any other living things are inescapably selfish. Genes are not literally selfish. Genes do not act. It is living things, biological organisms, the carriers of genes, that act, and the metaphor of 'the selfish gene' is part of an evolutionary explanation of why organisms tend to act as they do. The evolutionary process will tend to select those behavioural traits which perpetuate the organisms' genetic material rather than the individual organisms themselves. Consider two organisms competing for survival in the same habitat. One of them is more inclined to sacrifice its offspring for the sake of its own survival. The other is more inclined to sacrifice itself for its offspring at the cost of its own survival. It is clear that it is the offspring of the latter which are more likely to survive and in their turn reproduce, and hence the genetic coding which gives rise to the second kind of behaviour is to that extent more likely to be perpetuated than that which gives rise to the first. That is the point of the 'selfish gene' metaphor. It gives no reason to suppose that human beings or any other living things will be inescapably selfish. On the contrary, it explains why 'kin altruism', self-sacrificing behaviour for the sake of one's offspring or other genetic relatives, may be selected for.

That confirms what we know from everyday experience of

human life. Of course individual human beings can some-times act in appallingly selfish ways, but there is no inevit-ability about this. The primary problem for moral motivation, I suggest, is not the problem of selfishness but the problem of *partial altruism*. What all too often drives people to do terrible things is a limited devotion to particular individuals or a par-ticular group. The gangster is driven by a code of vendetta to carry out revenge killings for the sake of the honour of his own gang. Besotted lovers will kill for the sake of those they love. The most ruthless and thuggish thieves and murderers will kill anyone who threatens their kids. On a larger scale, fanatics will commit appalling acts of war and terrorism, killing thousands for the sake of their own political cause or their religion or their nation. Suicide bombers may be terrify-ing, but the problem is not their selfishness, and if they were more selfish we might have less reason to be terrified.

As it stands, that is no great comfort. It does not give us reason to be sanguine about the prospect of people behaving well. It does however help us to get clearer about the nature of the problem. The examples of ruthless and fanatical behaviour to which I have referred are themselves confirmation of the claim I made earlier in this chapter – that human beings are *social* beings, who need to identify themselves with others. And it is these characteristics, I have argued, that give us at least the potential to be *moral* beings.

This can give us some hope. The fact of human nature which is the problem for moral motivation is also, at least potentially, the solution. Most human beings are capable of imaginative identification with others, of sensitivity to the joys and sufferings of others, and of being moved by that awareness. That is, potentially, a capacity to be moved by the joys and sufferings of *anyone*, but most human beings live within a narrow circle. The only antidote, therefore, is that of a wider experience. It is when we encounter the 'other', and recognise that he or she, whom we had excluded as less than fully human, as an alien outsider, whom we had stereotyped as 'the enemy' or 'the infidel' or 'the savage', is a human being like oneself, that moral insight dawns. This can happen most strikingly through a direct encounter – through being brought face to face with one's potential victim, for instance – but it can also happen in other ways, such as through imaginative literature which awakens us to the texture of other people's lives, or through good news reporting and journalism which awakens us to the plight of others. There is no guarantee that this will happen, but it is the possibility to which human beings are at least open, and it is the possibility which gives us moral hope.

REMOVING THE CLUTTER

I have argued both that a rational morality need not rest on the authority of religion, and that in practice people have the psychological resources to live a good life without needing to be motivated by divine commands. I have argued that there are shared human values grounded in human nature. Those values, therefore, are not the exclusive preserve of humanists. It is no surprise that they feature in the moral codes of the various different religions, and that there is extensive common ground between religious and humanist moralities, reflecting these shared values. Nevertheless, humanist morality does not leave everything as it was. Religious moralities typically combine these shared human values with a good deal of clutter, and humanists will want to remove the clutter.

That means, first, that humanists will want to reject moral injunctions which have no basis other than a religious one. I mentioned at the beginning of this chapter moral prohibitions which take the form of appeals to scriptural authority, and gave the example of the condemnation of homosexuality in *Leviticus*. As a matter of fact the irrational elements in religious moralities typically have to do with sexual activity, and as well as being backed by the quoting of scriptural texts they are often also defended with claims of privileged insight into the intentions of a divine creator. The Roman Catholic Church, for instance, continues to oppose all contraceptive methods, on the grounds that they render the sexual act incapable of performing its natural and divinely ordained purpose of procreation. Notoriously, the influence of the Catholic Church in this matter has been an enormous obstacle to attempts to stop the spread of AIDS.

The Anglican Church in Britain does not take the same line on contraception, but it is convulsed by conflict about homosexuality. When, in 2003, it was proposed that a gay man should be appointed as a bishop, this provoked bitter opposition and the prospective bishop was forced to stand down; and when in the same year a gay man was made a bishop in the Episcopal Church in the United States, this threatened to create a deep split in the Anglican communion world-wide. The argument of the opponents of homosexuality is again a claim about the proper purpose of sexuality, formulated as a claim about God's intentions in creation.

> The Church's understanding of scripture and of long-standing tradition is that the proper place for sexual relationships is within marriage. This is based on the order of Creation where men and women are seen as complementary. Sexual intercourse, within the life-long relationship of marriage, is the sign and beautiful expression of that

union. Intercourse outside marriage undermines the power of that sign.[16]

So whereas the Catholics think that God gave us sex to be confined to the function of reproduction, the Anglicans think that God gave us sex to be a 'sign and beautiful expression' of the complementarity of men and women.

How do they know? What possible grounds can there be for saying that, of the many different purposes which sexuality can serve in human life, some of them, or perhaps only one, are the ones which God intended and the rest are therefore impermissible? For myself, I should want to attribute more generous intentions to the Almighty. I should prefer to believe that if there were a god, his reasons for giving us not only genital organs but also oral and anal orifices might have been to diversify the sources of sexual enjoyment and thereby make them accessible to gays as well as to heterosexuals. However, in the absence of a god, I can, from a humanist perspective, see no rational grounds for objecting to gay sex. It is true that if all human sexual activity were exclusively homosexual the human species would soon die out – but that is scarcely a serious danger.

MORAL COMPLEXITY: EUTHANASIA AND ABORTION

One way, then, in which a humanist morality will differ from a religious one is that it will reject any components of the latter which have no rational foundation, in particular those which are based solely on alleged scriptural authority, or on claims to a knowledge of divine purposes which, even if there were a god, could never be sustained. A second difference is that those shared values which are common to humanist and religious moralities will sometimes be interpreted differently.

In particular, if moral values are seen as emanating from divine commands, there is a tendency to treat them dogmatically, as simple general rules which have to be adhered to whatever the circumstances. I do not want to caricature religious believers; there are plenty of them whose moral thinking is as sensitive and as nuanced and as alert to the complexities as any secular thinking could be. Nevertheless, as an example of the tendency I have in mind, consider the attitude of the Catholic Church towards voluntary euthanasia.

> euthanasia is a grave violation of the law of God, since it is the
> deliberate and morally unacceptable killing of a human
> person. This doctrine is based upon the natural law and upon
> the written word of God.[17]

This comes from a papal encyclical letter on the moral implications of 'the value and inviolability of human life'. It is good that it takes that value seriously, but it also does so simplistically, both in its discussion of abortion (which I will consider shortly) and in its discussion of euthanasia. Its verdict on the latter is the conclusion of a simple syllogism: euthanasia is the killing of an innocent human being, the killing of an innocent human being is always wrong, therefore euthanasia is always wrong. That simple syllogism is too simple. The complexities are apparent to most people, and they are a good illustration of those main features of humanist morality which I previously identified. Of course the deliberate taking of human life is normally a terrible wrong. The circumstances in which the question of euthanasia arises, however, are typically those where a person is dying, in terrible pain, and for whom there is no prospect other than that of continued suffering until it is relieved by death. The case for euthanasia is therefore, in part, grounded in the attitude of *care*, the desire to relieve a person's suffering. That, however, is not by itself a sufficient justification. If a person dying in pain wills to go on fighting, struggling to go on despite the pain, then their courage and their choice are to be respected, for it is their life and it is therefore for them to choose their manner of dying. By the same token, however, someone whose choice is to end their pain, to have their life ended because it no longer offers any prospect but that of pointless suffering, has the same claim to have their wishes respected, because it is their life. The desire to end it will typically be not just a desire to be released from the physical pain, but a wish to die with *dignity*, to end one's life not just as an empty shell, a body drugged senseless, but as a human being still at the end capable of making choices and of choosing one's manner of dying. The papal encyclical sometimes formulates its case against euthanasia by saying that a law permitting euthanasia would be 'in complete opposition to the inviolable right to life proper to every individual'.[18] I have noted previously the possibility of putting the idea of respect for life in the language of 'rights'. But part of the point of that language is to emphasise that, in virtue of having rights, people have choices, that their autonomy should be respected, and that includes being able to choose whether or not to exercise their rights. To say that I have a right to life is to say that it is my life, mine to preserve but also mine to end. That is why, in the moral argument about euthanasia, there is all the difference between *voluntary* euthanasia, which respects people's right to life, and *involuntary* euthanasia, that is, euthanasia against the person's own wishes, which would clearly be an intolerable violation of the right to life.

Many humanists, therefore, because they locate the ideas of the value of life and the right to life within the wider context of care for people's well-being and respect for people's autonomy, recognise a case for making voluntary euthanasia legally permissible. That, however, is not the end of the argument. If there is a case in principle for changing the law in that way, there are also difficult questions about the practicalities and the wider long-term consequences of doing so. In particular there are proper concerns about the dangers of a 'slippery slope'. If voluntary euthanasia were legally permitted, would the elderly and infirm then come under pressure to say that they wanted their lives to be ended, because they did not wish to be 'a burden', and would voluntary euthanasia turn imperceptibly into involuntary euthanasia? Would it be possible in practice for the legalisation of voluntary euthanasia to incorporate firm safeguards to prevent this from happening? For my own part I think that such safeguards are possible, and that the slope need not be slippery, but I am not concerned to argue that here. I simply want to emphasise again the inescapable complexity of the moral argument, and the inadequacy of appeals to simple general rules, whether the rule in question is that of never deliberately ending a human life or that of always respecting people's choices.

Similar divisions, between an over-simplifying religious morality and the complexity on which humanists will want to insist, are illustrated by a second controversial example, the argument about abortion. Again I do not want to caricature the views of religious believers. Some, I know, take an appropriately nuanced approach to the question, but some think that all the dilemmas and difficulties are covered by a simple general rule, and their adherence to this rule is explicitly linked by them to their belief in the divine authority which underpins it. Abortion, they say, is always murder, and is therefore always wrong. Life is a gift from God and we must never destroy it. To do so would be to violate the divine commandment 'Thou shalt not kill'. This is the position taken by the Roman Catholic Church (as illustrated by the papal encyclical to which I have already referred), and it is taken also by some other Christian groups as well as some Jews and Muslims.

How does it over-simplify the problem? Let us first note some common-sense reasons in support of the obvious idea that birth is a morally significant watershed. Birth is – as some philosophers would put it – the beginning of the child's 'being in the world'. The new-born baby encounters a world of objects with which she must interact, and which she immediately tries to manipulate, beginning with the most rudimentary attempts to suck at the mother's breast and thereby obtain satisfaction and comfort. In attempting to manipulate and control things in the world the child immediately begins to build up an awareness of her environment, as something having an order and structure, containing obstacles and rewards. The world which she encounters is also a social world, one in which there are other human beings who respond to her and to whom in turn she learns to respond, who encourage some of her responses and discourage others, so that her simple biological reflexes begin to become patterns of behaviour. Only from birth can we meaningfully speak of the child learning to *act* and to become *conscious* of things and to *want* things and to *interact* with people. And the moral significance is that these are the things we value when we talk of valuing a human *life*.

Birth is, therefore, a moral divide, but that is not all that there is to be said, and we have not yet identified the real complexity. There is a difference between the child's being in the womb prior to birth and the child's being in the world after birth, but of course the child just before birth is biologically the same as the child just after birth. Therefore (although no woman is going to have an abortion at nine months) a very late abortion is *very like* killing a new-born baby. On the other hand, a very early abortion (performed, say, by taking a 'morning after' pill to prevent the fertilised egg from implanting in the womb), when the foetus is just a single cell or minute group of cells, is nothing like killing a new-born baby. And this is precisely what makes the abortion problem so difficult: an early abortion is not at all like murder, a late abortion is disturbingly like murder, and there is no clear cut-off point between those two extremes. The present position in British law, which sets a time limit before which abortion is permissible, is basically right, I think, but the time limit, though not totally arbitrary, is relatively so. There is no radical difference between the foetus at 24 weeks and the foetus at 25 weeks. The development of the foetus is a continuous process from conception to birth. We can call this 'the continuum problem', and it is the first reason why the question of abortion is more complex than the anti-abortionists recognise.

The anti-abortionists would of course dispute this. They would say that, from the moment of conception, the fertilised egg is a life, and that to destroy it, at any stage, is therefore murder. It is true, indeed, that the fertilised egg is a biologically living thing, but they then owe us an account of what distinguishes it from any other biologically living thing – any other single-celled organism, for instance – and makes it 'sacred'. The answer cannot be that, from conception, it has that unique DNA which makes it a unique individual, for the same is true of any other living thing. Is it the fact that the life in question is a *human* life? Then they owe us an account of why this makes it sacrosanct, since the fertilised egg has none of the features which we value in a human life, and the trouble with all these approaches is that they detach the concept of 'life' from everything that underpins our moral understanding of respect for human life.

What they may well say at this point is that the fertilised egg has the *potential* to become a human life in the full sense. Now the idea of potential is indeed relevant here, but it takes us in a very different direction from the idea of murder. As a man I do not want to pontificate about how women feel about abortions, but the thought of unrealised potential must be one reason why a woman's decision to have an abortion will be a difficult one. There is, I imagine, always likely to be that thought about what would have become of the child if the pregnancy had not been ended. But this is not at all like the thought of having killed someone. It is perhaps more akin to the thought of how the woman's children would have turned out if their father had been not Jack but Jim, who also wanted to marry her. Or if that seems too weak a comparison, perhaps it is akin to the thought of the woman who decides not to have children at all, but wonders what might have been, or the thought of the woman who gives her child up for adoption, but wonders how things would have worked out if she had kept it. None of these is a precise equivalent of the way in which an abortion prevents the realisation of a potential, but they are all examples of how a contemplation of 'what might have been' can be disturbing. The thought of unrealised potential is always troubling, and it may sometimes be morally troubling, but it is quite different from the thought of murder, and the difference between the two is a second element of complexity in the abortion question.

There is thirdly, of course, the complexity which consists

in the range of positive reasons why a woman might want to have an abortion. These will be many and various, but in essence they will come down to a woman's concerns about her own well-being, and about the well-being of the child, if she were to have one. The two kinds of concerns will often overlap, and that is one reason why concerns of the first kind cannot just be dismissed as 'selfish'. Some reasons for having an abortion might properly be regarded as trivial – if, for instance, a woman unexpectedly finds that she is pregnant and does not want to give up the holiday to which she has been looking forward. But if having a child will alter the whole course of a woman's life, will destroy all her plans for her career and her future, that is no trivial matter. If it means having to bring up a child on her own, in circumstances where she may lack the financial resources or the emotional resources to give it a decent chance in life, those will be strong reasons for having an abortion. And we should note that the question will often be not so much whether or not to have a child, but whether to have a child *now* or *later*, when she will be in a better position to care for it. So the third reason why the abortion question is a more complex matter than can be captured in any simple rule is that all these considerations come into play, and are rightly regarded as relevant. The anti-abortionists will say that, however much we may sympathise with the hardships of a woman who has a child in difficult circumstances, all these considerations are outweighed by the moral wrongness of killing. However, if the view of abortion as killing is itself too simple, then these other reasons will properly be regarded as parts of the total picture. A woman's decision about whether to have an abortion will then be a matter of weighing up all these relevant kinds of consider-ations – the stage the pregnancy has reached, how she will feel about the child that might have been, how good or bad the consequences of having the child or having the abortion will be. Sometimes the question will be relatively straight-forward, sometimes it will be difficult. That is why those who argue for the permissibility of abortion rightly insist on 'the woman's right to choose', for only she is in a position to take full account of all the particular complexities of her particular circumstances.

I cannot emphasise sufficiently strongly that many religious believers are sensitive to these complexities. Many, however, are not, and I think it fair to reiterate that they over-simplify the moral problem *because* they view it from a religious per-spective. The people who picket abortion clinics and threaten doctors, and who carry placards saying 'Abortion is murder', are very often Christians, and they very often say that they do it *because* they are Christians. They may be wrong about every-thing else, but I cannot deny that they are right about their own motivation.

The recognition of complexity is sometimes denounced as 'relativism', and that label is sometimes used to describe the abyss into which secular humanism would lead us and from which only a traditional religious morality can preserve us. I have noted previously that 'relativism' can mean various things. If it is the view that what is right and wrong is simply a matter of the attitudes and conventions prevailing at a par-ticular time in a particular society, then indeed relativism is to be rejected, and a humanist morality has nothing to do with relativism in this sense. However, the term 'relativism' is sometimes used to mark a contrast with the idea that moral rules are 'absolute', and this in turn is equated with the idea that simple rules such as that it is wrong to kill, or to steal, or to lie, or to break a promise, or to have sex outside marriage, should be observed without any exceptions, whatever the circumstances. Relativism in this sense would be the view that what we ought to do is 'relative to the particular circumstances'; that is to say, it will often depend on the details of the particular case, especially when different values are in conflict with one another. Because of the confusing ambiguity of the term I would prefer not to call this 'relativism'. (The term 'situationism' has sometimes been used as a better way of referring to such a position.) However, if that is what we mean by it here, then relativism is something we should embrace. Life is complex, and to ignore the complexity is not an admirable adherence to moral absolutes, it is morally irresponsible.

LOOKING FOR RIGHT ANSWERS

Those, then, are two ways in which the content of a humanist morality will differ from at least certain kinds of religious morality. It will exclude supposed moral values which rest on nothing more than appeals to scriptural authority or claims about the intended purposes of a divine creator. It will also interpret shared values as appropriately complex rather than as simple general rules. Apart from these differences of *content* there are, I think, two ways in which a humanist approach is likely to involve a distinctive position on the *status* of moral views. The first of these I have already mentioned – that humanists will see 'morality' not as a special institution which imposes its own special set of requirements, but as an aspect of the general question of how to live a good life. A good human life includes both individual fulfilment and responsibilities to others, and 'morality' may perhaps seem to go with the latter rather than the former component, but the two aspects cannot be separated, for an understanding of those responsibilities involves recognising how they all fit into a meaningful human life.

The second point about the status of moral judgements follows from my previous emphasis on complexity. It is a mistake to suppose that there is always a single right answer to every moral dilemma. Sometimes, perhaps often, there is. Often, when we are tempted to act badly, what is needed is simply that we should acknowledge the truth about what we ought to do, and stick to it. Sometimes, however, where conflicting values are finely balanced, there may be no truth of the matter as to which should carry the greater weight in the particular case. To suppose that there always is a right answer is, I suggest, a legacy of the idea of moral action as obedience to divine commands, and thus of moral judgement as a matter of second-guessing the mind of the divine commander.

Moral conflicts to which there is no solution may be cases of what can be called *moral tragedy* – cases in which we have to choose between outcomes each of which is appalling, and where there is no evading our responsibility to choose. That might be the case in political contexts, for instance, where people sometimes face the choice of either submitting to intolerable oppression or seeking to end it by the use of violence which will mean the deaths of innocent people. But insoluble dilemmas are also faced by people in their everyday personal lives. Take the case of someone who is trying to decide whether to end a close personal relationship. Would it be an act of betrayal? Or would it be an honest recognition of the fact that the relationship is dead? Sometimes there *is* a right answer, even though the individual concerned may fail to see it. Blinded by the prospect of a new and younger partner, he or she may fail to see the superficiality of the new relationship, the enduring value of the old, and the pain that will be caused. Or, blinded by inertia, he or she may persist in a misguided loyalty which constricts both their lives. But sometimes, to the question 'Is the relationship dead?', the only honest answer may be 'Well, it is and it isn't'. It is no less important to try to face reality honestly and clearly, but the complexity of that reality may defeat any attempt to reduce it to a manageable simplicity and thus to arrive at a determinate decision.

Am I here reverting to what I earlier called 'crude subjectivism'? No. The trouble with the crude subjectivist position is that it denies that there are right answers to *any* moral questions. It thereby obliterates the vital distinction between those cases where answers are available and those where they are not. By abandoning the legacy of the 'divine commands' model, we can resist the idea that there will *always* be right answers. But by recognising the fact of shared human values, we can also see the need to search honestly for the truth about what we ought to do and how we ought to live, we can use our rationality and our capacity for imaginative identification in the search for answers, and we can expect that we shall sometimes be able to find them and to live by them.

Five

Looking back on the previous chapters, I cannot escape the feeling that everything that I have said is obvious. Certainly there is nothing philosophically innovative in it. Though there are academic philosophers who subscribe to religious beliefs, the criticisms which I have rehearsed against the traditional arguments for the existence of God are standard ones. Likewise the accounts of why scientific method is a reliable source of knowledge, and why scientific understanding does not exclude familiar beliefs about the distinctive characteristics of human beings, seem to me to be fairly uncontroversial. Most moral philosophers would agree that morality is logically independent of religion, and though the debates between subjectivism and objectivism, and between utilitarianism, Kantianism and other positions remain contested, my discussion covers familiar ground. Moreover, the feeling of obviousness is not just a matter of philosophical familiarity. I am also inclined to think that the broad position which I have defended is largely a matter of common sense.

That view sits uneasily alongside the recognition that most of what I have had to say would be rejected by most human beings, now and throughout history. In previous eras those who have rejected religious belief have been a tiny minority, and although in our own society religion has lost much of its hold on popular belief – this has indeed been a revolutionary shift in attitudes over the past century – it is still the case that most people in most societies are religious. If that commits me to the conclusion that the majority of human beings have failed to recognise truths which have the status of obvious common sense, perhaps that should also lead me to a rather pessimistic view of human rationality.

The sense of obviousness could however be given a different gloss, for it might be alleged that the positions which I have defended are not so much *obvious* as *banal*. They may seem to invite the charge that a humanist view of the world is essentially *shallow*. Its limitations, perhaps, are the limitations of a scientific rationalism which claims to explain everything and which, in its overweening self-confidence, leaves no room for depth or mystery. It is a charge often summed up by saying that humanism leaves no room for the *spiritual* dimension of human life. What are we to make of such charges? In attempting to rebut them, in this final chapter, I shall take a more personal approach than I have done previously. The views which I have defended in earlier chapters, though not a humanist orthodoxy, are ones which would probably meet with a broad consensus of agreement from a great many secular humanists. In the remaining pages of the book I am going to talk about how it is possible for a humanist to find life enriching and meaningful. The topic is by its nature a more personal one, and the suggestions which I am going to make are personal ones.

THE SENSE OF MYSTERY

Let us look first at the accusation that humanism, insofar as it is wedded to scientific rationalism, excludes a sense of mystery. There is no need for a humanist to deny that the universe is mysterious and that it will ultimately elude human understanding. To say that detailed and methodical scientific investigation and, more broadly, rational thought and argument are the tools we have for understanding the world is not to say that they will enable us to understand everything. Indeed, the recognition that human beings are, like every other species, a product of evolution can be one source of an appropriate modesty. From our human standpoint we can see that the sensory and intellectual capacities even of species close to us in the evolutionary sequence are limited, so that there are features of the world which they could not possibly understand, and it is a reasonable inference that there are comparable limitations to human understanding. No intelligent chimpanzee will ever understand Newton's laws of motion, or debate philosophical questions about the nature of consciousness or the status of morality, or appreciate the intricate construction of a Bach fugue. By the same token there must presumably be aspects of reality which no human being will ever understand. We know that the human species is not a species set apart, with a privileged status, made in the image of God, but is like every other species a product of biological history. Like every other species we are limited by our physical constitution. We are limited to the perceptual and intellectual capacities which are dependent on our sensory organs and the structure of our brains. We can therefore assume that there are features of the world which our biological make-up excludes us from understanding, and others which we can only dimly grasp. Think of the limited understanding which a dog has of the factors which determine when it is fed and when it is taken for a walk. It has certain expectations, but it is constitutionally precluded from understanding why those expectations are often warranted and will sometimes be upset. If there were beings with a different kind of intelligence from our own, the limitations of human understanding might be analogously apparent to them.

I must emphasise that I am not implying that there are such beings. Still less am I implying that the limits of human understanding point to the existence of any divine intelligence. My point is a negative one, and it is essential that the grounds for intellectual modesty remain modest. If religious believers insist on reminding a humanist philosopher that 'there are more things in heaven and earth than are dreamt of in your philosophy',[1] they are almost certainly right. To that extent the sense of mystery is an aspect of the religious stance for which I have every respect. We must however resist the temptation to turn it into an appeal to non-rational insight. The claim to do justice to the sense of mystery sits uneasily alongside the claims of the organised religions to have all the answers. The disparity is especially incongruous when we consider the dogmatic certainties on which the orthodox religious systems are bound to insist. The dominant religion of our own culture takes it to be quite certain that its founder died and then returned to life three days later. Such a claim is one whose inherent improbability would have to be countered by a wealth of extremely well-documented evidence in order to have any plausibility at all, and yet no one can call himself or herself a Christian unless he or she accepts this claim as an incontrovertible truth. Not much room there for modesty in respect of human cognitive powers. Dogmatic certainty of this kind, promulgated by the organised religions, extends to questions which by any normal reckoning would be regarded as trivial or meaningless. Who was the greatest of the prophets, Moses or Jesus or Mohammed? The question is about as significant as university league tables, or polls to decide who was the greatest Briton of all time, yet the world remains riven by the conflicting claims. As for the question of whether the seventh day, on which the creator of the universe rested and on which he therefore wants us to worship him, was a Friday, a Saturday or a Sunday, this question, central to the religious identity of millions of people, is literally meaningless.

I am not trying to score cheap points. I take very seriously the need for a sense of mystery. It is important to establish that humanism can accommodate it, and indeed can foster it more genuinely than do the institutionalised religions. Nor is it just a matter of recognising our intellectual limitations. It is a matter also of having an appropriate sense of awe and wonder when confronted with the vastness and complexity of the natural universe. Again a scientific rationalism can promote this rather than dispel it. Humans have, for instance, always felt a sense of awe when contemplating the night sky. How much more so, now that we know more about the vastness of interstellar space and the huge distances from which the light of the stars has travelled. Religions, then, have no monopoly on the emotional dimension of the sense of mystery.[2] And its intellectual dimension, the recognition of the limitations of human understanding, is more readily reconcilable with humanist than with religious beliefs.

SPIRITUALITY

What about the wider charge, that humanism excludes the *spiritual* dimension? I have to confess that I am quite uncertain about what is meant by 'spirituality'. It is a word which I distrust. It is inherently slippery. If you say that you do not need spirituality and do not recognise it, you risk incurring the charge of superficiality. You appear to confine life to the shallow and the trivial. If you say that you of course recognise the importance of the spiritual side of life, you risk being told that you are really 'religious' after all. The word works to monopolise depth and seriousness on behalf of an other-worldly religiosity.

For that reason I am inclined not to use the word. However, let us take our cue from the implied contrast between spirituality and shallowness. If the word 'spiritual' is thought to point to something important, which we are in danger of missing, then let us ask what it is that gives depth to human life. What are the things that 'lift the spirit', the things that make us want to go on, that make life worth living? And does humanism exclude them?

Of course not. Again we risk descending into banality, but I think we all know from experience what these things are. Here are some of them.

The satisfaction of creative achievement: We want to make our mark on the world, to make a difference to it, by producing something that puts our plans and intentions into effect. We want to be able to look at something and say 'I did that – that's me'. If we are lucky, we may get this satisfaction from the work which we do to earn our living. Some people get it from artistic creativity, from painting or writing or music-making. Others get it from so-called 'leisure activities', such as decorating the house or making a garden, which are not just ways of filling the time but provide a real sense of achievement.

The excitement of discovery: 'All human beings,' says Aristotle, 'by nature desire to know.'[3] We seek knowledge not just as a means to an end, but for its own sake. Driven by a sense of wonder, of curiosity, we derive deep satisfaction from solving a problem or coming to understand what was previously puzzling. Scientific enquiry, historical research and philosophical argument are more formal examples of an excitement which can be experienced by anyone.

Relationships with others: I have referred previously to Aristotle's description of human beings as *social* beings. This is not just a fact about our biology and our need for cooperation in order to survive, but a fact about our emotional needs. We need one another. Though we differ in the degree to which we may enjoy being alone, no one wants to be lonely. More positively, we know the delight of getting to know another person, discovering shared interests and enthusiasms as well as being intrigued by the other's differences and idiosyncrasies. We take pleasure in and are uplifted by the company and support of others.

The life of the emotions: To talk of such relationships is to talk of our emotional life, and first and foremost the emotion of love in its myriad forms – the love of friends, the love of parents and children, and sexual love in all its variety from casual encounters to enduring partnerships. It is not just the positive emotions, however, of love and of joy and delight, but the negative emotions also which are essential to a rich life – the emotions of doubt and fear, of anger and hatred. Though the immediate experience may be something we would wish to avoid, such emotions are all essential to the complex texture of our lives. How could there be a full life in which there were no fears and doubts to overcome, no anger at hypocrisy and injustice and no hatred of those who perpetrate it?

The enjoyment of beauty in art and nature: I refer here to 'beauty' in a wide sense, not just the 'pretty', but the beauty of a desolate wilderness or of gentle rain or a violent thunderstorm or a valley shrouded in mist. I use the word 'beauty' to encompass all the stimulation which we derive from the arts, including that which shocks or disturbs. Such experience is clearly linked with the experience of emotions and the capacity of the arts to convey them and explore them, including the emotions of pain and desolation. There is also the enjoyment of the beauty of the human form, again encompassing not just the stereotypically pretty but the beauty of a face in which a life is made visible.

These, we know, are the things which enrich our experience. There would be no need to state the obvious, were it not for the suggestion that a life without religion and religious 'spirituality' is somehow impoverished. Why then might it be thought that these things are not enough?

They may be felt not to be enough because they are *fragile*. Creativity may be elusive because our projects may fail. The excitement of discovery can only to a limited degree be achieved unaided; it depends on others to educate and guide and inform us, and the resources may not be there. Fulfilling relationships may be hard to come by, because of the accidents of life or our own failure to surmount the barriers of shyness and self-doubt. The life of the emotions may be too hard to bear, because there is too much pain and suffering, especially in a life blighted by tragic loss or rejection or loneliness. The enjoyment of beauty may be unavailable to someone who lives in an ugly world and who simply lacks the means of access to the arts or to a more uplifting environment. Thus we are led to look for something more permanent. We seek a guarantee of spiritual depth which is reliable because it is built into the nature of the universe and is immune to the vicissitudes of time and chance and human weakness. This problem of fragility is one to which I shall return.

The second reason why the things which we know can enrich our lives may not be enough is that they may seem not to add up to anything. Any or all of them may be present, and yet life may still seem empty and pointless. It is the problem of the *meaning* of life. For many, religion provides that meaning. It purports to reveal how the life of the individual fits into an overall divine plan or purpose. It provides a general theoretical account of the nature and origin of the universe and of our place in it, of a kind which seems capable also of giving a shape and structure and purpose to the lives of individuals. It is therefore not surprising that religious believers often claim that *only* religion can do this, and that a life without religious faith is a life condemned to meaninglessness.

NARRATIVES AND MEANINGFUL LIVES

I want now to address this criticism that, without religious belief, human life lacks meaning and purpose. I shall argue that the arts, and especially literature and the other narrative arts, can and do fill this role which religion claims exclusively to fill. In fact I want to make a stronger claim than that. The arts are not just a substitute for traditional religion, a second-rate or scaled-down version of religion pressed into service to fill the gap left by secularisation. On the contrary, religious belief is itself just a special case of the way in which narratives, stories, shape our lives and give them meaning.[4] In arguing for this claim I shall be making another link between secular humanism and the older tradition of what I have called 'cultural humanism' – the idea that literature and the other arts are valuable not just as self-contained pursuits but because of the way in which they can help us in thinking about how we should live.

Philosophers of art tend to be suspicious of such claims, because they seem to reduce art to a purely instrumental role. I referred just now to the fact that the enjoyment and experience of the arts can enrich our lives. That is a familiar fact, but many people would go on to say that it is important to identify the distinctive kind of experience involved. To appreciate art *as art* is to enjoy a uniquely *aesthetic* experience, they might say – the enjoyment of *art for art's sake* – and we should not debase this experience by turning art into a tool for more mundane purposes. Someone who enjoys a piece of music because it reminds them of the romantic occasion on which they first heard it, or who reads a novel or watches a film or a play with a tragic theme because they like a good cry, or who enjoys a Constable landscape because it looks like the place where they had a relaxing country holiday and gives them a feeling of peace and tranquillity, is turning the work into a mere vehicle for emotional self-indulgence. Carried away by their emotions, they are failing to appreciate the work itself, as a work of art. Likewise someone who looks to a work of art or literature for a moral message, or to convey a political ideology and move people to political action, is turning it into mere propaganda. This attitude may appear intolerably snooty, but there is a serious point here. Our appreciation of the value of art is an appreciation of something unique and distinctive, and to treat art simply as a stimulus to the emotions or a means of conveying a message is to ignore that distinctive character and make art replaceable and hence dispensable. If the Constable landscape conjures up feelings of the peaceful countryside, then it would be even better to go and sit on the banks of the River Stour itself, dispense with the picture and enjoy the real thing. If the point of a film or a play is to extract a moral or political message, then why not go straight to the message and save time and effort?

My suggestion that the arts, and especially the narrative arts, enable us to give a meaning to our lives, by shaping our experience, may seem open to this objection. I want to defend my claim by showing that the arts do this in a distinctive way. They enable us to make sense of our lives, in a way in which nothing else can. This account of the arts, then, does not make them replaceable and dispensable. It is what is special and valuable about art, *as art*. I want to claim that to appreciate *aesthetic form*, the qualities of a work which make it aesthetically satisfying, is at the same time to recognise ways of shaping and giving a significant structure to our own experience.

I want to illustrate this claim with two literary examples. These are two novels which are both, directly and self-consciously, about the connection between form in art and form in life. In this respect they are atypical, and my use of them to support a *general* claim about that connection may look like cheating. However, they both practise what they preach. They both demonstrate in practice how literary form has a significance which goes beyond the work itself, a significance which is a matter of giving shape and meaning to our day-to-day experience. They therefore serve for me a dual purpose, of articulating explicitly the claim which I want to make, and of exemplifying it.

The first is Virginia Woolf's novel *To the Lighthouse*. It has an immediately obvious and distinctive formal structure. Woolf refers to it in her preparatory notes as 'two blocks joined by a corridor'.[5] The first of the two main parts – the first 'block' – is set in the holiday house of Mr and Mrs Ramsay in the

Hebrides, with their family and house guests. The project of sailing to the lighthouse, about which their young son James is intensely excited, is called off by Mr Ramsay because the weather will not be sufficiently fine. The bridging passage – the 'corridor' – describes, in impersonal terms, the passing of ten years, in which Mrs Ramsay dies, the First World War intervenes and the house is shut up and then re-opened. The second main part sees Mr Ramsay and the two children, James and Cam, sail to the lighthouse, completing the trip which had been aborted ten years earlier.

Those are the bare bones of the formal structure. As I have said, aesthetic form is also an explicit theme of the novel. One of the house guests, Lily Briscoe, is in the first part of the novel struggling to achieve the right balance in the picture she is painting. In the second part, she restarts the painting, and sees what is needed to complete it. So the aborted and then the successful struggle with the picture parallels the aborted and then the successful trip to the lighthouse, and the final sentence describing the completion of the picture also constitutes the completion of the novel itself and a kind of closure on the events and relationships with which it is concerned.

A preoccupation with aesthetic form is thus both implicit and explicit in the novel. But what does the novel's own form signify? Any novelist can write a novel which has the structure of two blocks linked by a bridging passage. The test of the *success* of this formal structure is its human significance. The balance between the two halves is the counterposing of Mrs Ramsay alive to Mrs Ramsay dead, and the way in which, in both cases, the lives of others revolve around her. She has the capacity to bring people together, and she herself, in this way, gives shape to people's lives. The structure of the novel also says something about continuity over time, the continuity between life and death and the significance which a person's life can have after they are dead.

There are two passages where the shaping influence of Mrs Ramsay on those around her is most apparent. The great set piece of the first half of the novel is the description of a dinner party. Mrs Ramsay begins in a mood of weariness.

> But what have I done with my life? thought Mrs. Ramsay, taking her place at the head of the table, and looking at all the plates making white circles on it. 'William, sit by me,' she said. 'Lily,' she said, wearily, 'over there.' . . . At the far end, was her husband, sitting down, all in a heap, frowning. What at? She did not know. She did not mind. She could not understand how she had ever felt any emotion or any affection for him. She had a sense of being past everything, through everything, out of everything, as she helped the soup, as if there was an eddy – there – and one could be in it, or one could be out of it, and she was out of it.
>
> (pp. 90–1)

But as the dinner progresses we see her deftness in bringing people into relation with one another. As it grows dark and the candles are lit, 'the faces on both sides of the table were brought nearer by the candle-light, and composed, as they had not been in the twilight, into a party round a table' (p. 106). Mrs Ramsay reflects on the transformation as she serves the casserole.

> Nothing need be said; nothing could be said. There it was, all round them. It partook, she felt, carefully helping Mr. Bankes to a specially tender piece, of eternity; as she had already felt about something different once before that afternoon; there is a coherence in things, a stability; something, she meant, is

immune from change, and shines out (she glanced at the
window with its ripple of reflected lights) in the face of the
flowing, the fleeting, the spectral, like a ruby; so that again
tonight she had the feeling she had had once today already, of
peace, of rest. Of such moments, she thought, the thing is
made that remains for ever after. This would remain.

(p. 114)

The passage is paralleled by another, in the second main part
of the novel, in which Lily Briscoe remembers Mrs Ramsay's
capacity to bring people together, and the memory is the vin-
dication of Mrs Ramsay's thought that 'something remains'.

When she thought of herself and Charles throwing ducks and
drakes and of the whole scene on the beach, it seemed to
depend somehow upon Mrs. Ramsay sitting under the rock,
with a pad on her knee, writing letters. . . . That woman sitting
there, writing under the rock resolved everything into
simplicity; made the angers, irritations fall off like old rags;
she brought together this and that and then this, and so made
out of that miserable silliness and spite . . . something – this
scene on the beach for example, this moment of friendship
and liking – which survived, after all these years, complete, so
that she dipped into it to re-fashion her memory of him, and it
stayed in the mind almost like a work of art.

'Like a work of art,' she repeated, looking from her canvas
to the drawing-room steps and back again. . . . And, resting,
looking from one to the other vaguely, the old question which
traversed the sky of the soul perpetually, the vast, the general
question which was apt to particularise itself at such
moments as these . . . stood over her, paused over her,
darkened over her. What is the meaning of life? That was
all – a simple question; one that tended to close in on one with

years. The great revelation had never come. . . . Instead there
were little daily miracles, illuminations, matches struck
unexpectedly in the dark. . . . Mrs. Ramsay bringing them
together . . . Mrs. Ramsay making of the moment something
permanent (as in another sphere Lily herself tried to make of
the moment something permanent) – this was of the nature
of a revelation. In the midst of chaos there was shape; this
eternal passing and flowing (she looked at the clouds going
and the leaves shaking) was struck into stability.

(pp. 175–6)

So Mrs Ramsay, in both halves of the novel, has this ability to
nurture the flow of sympathy between people and thereby
bring them as close as one can come to answering the question 'What is the meaning of life?' The meaning is to be
found not in some great revelation, some definitive doctrine,
but in these elusive moments when things come together. The
vision is never final and definitive, it always has to be re-
created, but it is these moments of illumination that sustain
us. The shape which they give to experience is like the form
of a work of art, like the way in which a painting traps into
stillness our constantly changing visual experience. And this
comparison between life and art is more than just an analogy,
for it is such works – including To the Lighthouse itself – which
educate our ability to find the shapes and the patterns. The
novel, in other words, does for us what Mrs Ramsay does for
people. It brings to mind how our experiences, and our relations with others, can fit together in the right kinds of ways to
form a satisfying and meaningful whole.

My second literary example is Graham Swift's novel
Waterland.[6] It is a novel about bleak lives, set in a bleak landscape,
that of the Fens. Its form is fragmented and episodic, moving

to and fro in time and in style, and its structure reflects the struggle to create a coherent story out of these lives of pain and frustration. Its narrator, Tom Crick, is a history teacher, who is being forced into retirement. He and his wife Mary are childless. She has suffered a mental breakdown, she has snatched a baby from its pram, she says that God sent her the baby, and she has been hospitalised. The novel reconstructs the stories of their lives, their family histories and the larger history of the Fen country, which make some sense of the bleak outcome. It tells the story of Tom and Mary's childhood friendship and juvenile sexual explorations resulting in the pregnancy and the botched abortion which made future child-bearing impossible. The larger history, whose episodes are interspersed with the personal story, is that of the drain-ing of the Fens and the commercial exploitation of the Fenland waterways, and that in turn is the backdrop to the history of Tom's mother's family and the rise and decline of their business fortunes. What emerges, two-thirds of the way through the novel, is the incestuous relationship between Tom's mother and grandfather, set against the disillusion engendered by the First World War. That relationship leads to the birth of the child whom the father, a recluse who has turned his back on the world and is losing touch with reality, believes will grow up to be 'a Saviour of the World'. This Saviour is Tom's mentally retarded older half-brother Dick, whose death is the climax of the novel and whose fate is linked with those of Tom and Mary.

The struggle of Tom, as the novel's narrator, to make sense of his life is thus the struggle to tell a coherent story, one which is both an impersonal history and a personal narrative, and which invokes archetypes from Greek tragedy (with its myths of incest and a doomed family line) and Christian

147 **The meaning of life and the need for stories**

imagery (the death of the Saviour). The need for stories, which is also the need for history, is an explicit and central theme of the novel.

> For my father, as well as being a superstitious man, had a knack for telling stories. Made-up stories, true stories; soothing stories, warning stories; stories with a moral or with no point at all; believable stories and unbelievable stories; stories which were neither one thing nor the other. It was a knack which ran in his family. But it was a knack which my mother had too – and perhaps he really acquired it from her. Because when I was small it was my mother who first told me stories, which, unlike my father, she got from books as well as out of her head, to make me sleep at night.
>
> (pp. 1–2)

The need for stories is also, for Tom Crick, the history teacher in a school where history is being 'cut back', the need for history. It is a need which he tries to vindicate to a class of cynical adolescents who are conscious that they may be at the end of history if the human race destroys itself in a nuclear war.

> Old Cricky, your history teacher, had already in one sense and of his own accord, ceased to teach history. In the middle of explaining how, with a Parisian blood-letting, our Modern World began, he breaks off and starts telling – these stories. Something about living by a river, something about a father who trapped eels, and a drowned body found in the river, years ago. And then it dawned on you: old Cricky was trying to put himself into history; old Cricky was trying to show you that he himself was only a piece of the stuff he taught.
>
> (pp. 4–5)

Why are the need for stories and the need for history such

deep needs? There are recurrent passages in the novel which offer explicit answers to that question, answers offered by Tom to his pupils.

> Children, only animals live entirely in the Here and Now. Only nature knows neither memory nor history. But man – let me offer you a definition – is the story-telling animal. Wherever he goes he wants to leave behind not a chaotic wake, not an empty space, but the comforting marker-buoys and trail-signs of stories.
>
> (p. 53)

> And so long as we have this itch for explanations, must we not always carry round with us this cumbersome but precious bag of clues called History? Another definition, children: Man, the animal which demands an explanation, the animal which asks Why.
>
> (p. 92)

> History: a lucky dip of meanings. Events elude meaning, but we look for meanings. Another definition of Man: the animal who craves meaning – but knows.
>
> (p. 122)

This search for meaning, through the telling of stories, and the locating of them in a wider history, is enacted in the novel as Tom Crick seeks to tell the multi-layered story which might make sense of his own apparent failure of a life. Like *To the Lighthouse*, then, *Waterland* is both explicitly and implicitly about the relation between aesthetic form, especially narrative form, and the form of a life. And the fragmented and episodic form of the novel epitomises the struggle to give form to our lives, the recalcitrance of experiences which seem messy and pointless and appear to add up to a life of futility and failure. If the novel is successful, it is because the apparently arbitrary and disorganised sequences of chapters and events gradually fall into place, and this counts as success because we can recognise in it the way in which the memories of any life can be given a significant shape.

I have suggested that it is especially the *narrative* arts that perform this shaping role. My examples have been two novels, but it is not just serious literature that plays this role, and it is not confined to 'high culture'. We are in fact bombarded with narratives, stories, from many directions and sources, and they all make claims on us as patterns with which to order our experience. As children we are told stories, and they already play this vital role of helping us to make sense of an otherwise confusing world. As adults we are constantly being fed stories, through films, television 'soap operas' and other dramas, and the continuing consumption of popular fiction is further evidence that the insatiable need for stories is matched by a seemingly limitless supply. Film, television and popular fiction all provide us with sample narratives for understanding our own lives.

To acknowledge the variety of sources of such narratives is to acknowledge also that their function can be performed well or badly. There are better and worse stories and not just any one will do. Especially if we include the narratives of popular culture, they are full of simplifications and stereotypes. Applying fictional narratives to our own lives therefore needs to be a two-way process. Drawing on the available narratives we can see our own experience in new and significant ways, but we can also draw on our experience to criticise defective narratives. We can identify with stories and recognise 'Yes, that's how it is', but by the same token the recognition may be, and often may need to be, withheld. The appropriate response will often be the critical one, 'No, it's not like that.' We need to recognise the distorting stereotypes and the escapism and the fantasy for what they are. It is not just the narratives provided by popular culture, by escapist films and novels, that invite this response. Take the idea of romantic love, for instance, which pervades not just popular fiction and films but the tradition of the literary novel, and which is a classic case of the way in which people's articulation of their own experience draws on the available narratives. People may interpret their experiences of sexual and emotional attraction in terms of the standard narrative of a potential lifelong union between two people who are made for each other, who can share their lives and be everything to one another. When life does not work out like that, they perhaps conclude that they have simply got the wrong partner, when a better response might be to recognise the greater complexity of relationships and to criticise the simplifications of the romantic model. And to criticise the model would be to criticise the cultural narratives which convey it to us.

I would want to argue that this shaping role, enabling us to give a meaning to our experience, is not confined to the narrative arts. Music and the visual arts, though they do not in quite the same way provide models with which to understand our lives as a whole, may similarly illuminate our emotional and sensory experience. However, the attempt to argue for that suggestion here would take me too far afield, and I want instead to return to the two questions which I have left hanging. There is first the question whether the claim which I am making for the narrative arts distorts the true nature of aesthetic appreciation. The criticism was that, by treating the arts as vehicles through which to convey an understanding of the meaning of life, we demote them to an instrumental function, which could as well be performed by other means, and fail to appreciate art *as art*. My response is to argue that the role which I have assigned to the arts is a distinctive one, one to which they are uniquely fitted. The arts enable us to give meaning to our lives and our experience because of their focus on *particularity*. It is this that makes art different from moral and philosophical treatises, from therapeutic counselling and from 'self-help' books (and, as I shall suggest in a moment, from religious doctrines and homilies). An artwork, or at any rate a successful work, cannot be replaced by any other work, still less by something other than art. Notoriously, if you try to sum up in a statement or a piece of practical advice what we learn about life from a novel or a film, it comes out either as banal and obvious or as empty and unpersuasive. For instance, if we tried to formulate the 'message' of Tolstoy's *Anna Karenina*, it might be: 'A relationship cut off from the rest of society is doomed to failure.' The statement by itself leaves us cold. We may be puzzled by it. Or we may accept it and think it a mere platitude. It is only when we track Tolstoy's detailed account of the deterioration of Anna's relationship with Vronsky, and are convincingly shown how she is increasingly trapped into isolation and driven to the brink of madness, that we can appreciate precisely why and in what ways the statement is true. And there is no other means elaborating its truth, other than by telling the story. It is s that convinces us.

So this novel, and any narrative, gets its power from the sentation of particular individuals, living particular lives having particular experiences. At the same time, they are s and experiences with which we can *identify*. We can apply account to our own lives, we can recognise our own experiences in the fictional account, and that is how we can learn from the fictions. They have what I want to call *paradigmatic particularity*. With this phrase I want to capture the combination of the two facts: (1) that fictional narratives provide 'paradigms', examples or patterns which are generalisable and can illuminate and make sense of our own experience, but (2) that they can do so only because they are stories about particular individuals, and because this is what makes them convincing and brings them to life. This paradigmatic particularity, I am suggesting, is the distinctive feature of the arts, and it is why their capacity to give meaning to our lives does not make them replaceable and potentially redundant. It is what makes art *art*.

RELIGIOUS NARRATIVES AND THE MULTIPLICITY OF STORIES

I want to draw on this notion of 'paradigmatic particularity' to address the other question I left hanging: the competing claims of art and religion to tell us the meaning of life. To defend the importance of art rather than religion I can usefully refer to a lecture given by the Archbishop of Canterbury, his Dimbleby Lecture, in which he too talked about the need for stories.[7] I agree with much of what he says in the lecture, especially about the need for larger narratives in a society built around the making of isolated consumer choices in the market:

> When people make choices about the more distant future, about things that won't directly affect them as individuals, they do so presumably because they see their own choices here and now as part of a larger story that makes sense of their lives and gives them a context. This is the sort of thing you do if this is how you want to see the overall pattern of the

human world turning out. . . . So if you see your choices here and now in the context of a larger story, this is a way of giving some sort of shape or sense to your own life, some sort of continuity to it.

But then, as he would of course in his role as Archbishop, he moves to claims about the privileged status of religion in giving us the right story.

We need ways of getting a story straight so that we don't have to go on repeating it, repeating patterns of behaviour that never move us on. . . . All good therapy and counselling have something to do with this business of getting the story straight; but what is different about religious belief is its bold claim that there is a story of the whole universe without which your own story won't make sense.

There is a long tradition, from Matthew Arnold to the 'Sea of Faith' people, of reinterpreting religious belief as a collection of stories we can tell, stories with an imaginative rather than a literal truth.[8] But if that is all there is to religion, there is nothing special about it. We have any number of stories, and the ones which happen to be located in religious texts have no special status. Obviously the Archbishop wants to preserve that special status, he wants to say that the Christian narrative – presumably the narrative of the Creation, the Fall, the Incarnation and Resurrection and Redemption – is a privileged narrative. I can see why he wants to describe it as a narrative. To engage with people's lives and experience, it must do so in the manner of a story, a story which people can see themselves as part of. It must come alive. It is, perhaps, what postmodernists call a 'grand narrative', but it is of course more than a narrative. It is a body of doctrine. As such, it makes claims to literal truth, and indeed to having a monopoly on truth. If it is to vindicate the claim to a privileged status, therefore, it has got to be able to justify the traditional truth-claims that go with it – the doctrines of the divine creation of the universe, the incarnation, the resurrection of Jesus, and so forth. Naturally, I do not think that it can do so.

If the doctrine is abandoned, if the Christian narrative or any other religious narrative is offered simply as a story which can give shape to our lives, any claim to a privileged status must go by the board. There are any number of narratives on offer, and there is no reason why they have to be religious ones in order to play that role. Stories, I have suggested, do have to meet standards of truth. They have to fit our experience, and if they distort it then they have to be questioned. But stories need not be exclusive. Different stories make sense of different facets of our lives, and at different times, and we need the variety. Traditional religious stories are a part of that multiplicity. There are the parables told by Jesus, and the archetypal Old Testament stories such as the stories of the Garden of Eden and the Fall, the Flood, the Tower of Babel, the Exodus from Egypt and the search for the Promised Land. There are the central stories of the Christian faith: the Christmas story of mother and child and the birth in a lowly stable, and the story of the suffering of the saviour put to death. These are images deeply embedded in our culture; it would be crazy to want to jettison them, and they go on exerting their power just as do the stories of the gods and goddesses of the ancient Greeks. But they take their place alongside all the other narratives, equally compelling and illuminating, on which we draw.

The rejection of religious doctrine means also a rejection of the transcendent. Fictional narratives give meaning to our lives *from within*. They do not depend on any divine plan into which our individual lives fit, nor therefore do they provide any super-human guarantee against failure. This returns us to the problem of fragility. In talking previously of the concept of the 'spiritual', I listed the sorts of things which we value at a deep level and which can inspire us, but I acknowledged that they are all fragile. This is why people feel the need for the guarantees of permanence which religious belief may seem to provide insofar as it offers us a view of ourselves as part of a divine cosmic purpose. If that guarantee is not available, if all that we have are the stories that shape our experience, where does that leave the problem of fragility?

It leaves it as something which we have to accept. A meaningful life is not necessarily a good life. The narratives on which we draw may enable us to see a shape and a pattern in our lives, but there is no escaping the fact that the pattern may be one of failure. The human condition is one of vulnerability and we have to face the fact.[9] It has been said that the Christian world-view has no room in the end for the idea of *tragedy*, and I suspect that this is true of all the monotheistic religions, since they are bound to offer the consolation of ultimate salvation and redemption guaranteed by an omnipotent and benevolent god. The narrative of tragedy is one which we have inherited from the ancient Greeks and their messier view of the world as a chaotic playground of warring gods and goddesses none of whom holds any brief for human well-being. The great stories of tragedy in the literary tradition are a reminder that our fate may be terrible and that there may be no consolation. Humanism is not intrinsically a tragic world-view, but it is one which acknowledges the possibility of tragedy.

HUMANISM: FRAGILE, PROVISIONAL, AND PARTICULAR

This leads me to sum up the character of the humanism I want to defend, and to draw together the themes of my discussion. My humanism is one which accepts the fact of human *fragility*. It is a *provisional* humanism. And it is one which focuses on *particularity*.

To recognise *fragility* is to accept that we are vulnerable to circumstances. But we are also vulnerable to our own failings. Just as there are no guarantees provided by a divine plan that all will be well in the end, so also there are no guarantees in human nature that we will through our own resources be able to create a perfect world. Just as we have to acknowledge that terrible things can happen to us, so also we have to acknowledge that we can do terrible things. That was why, in my introductory chapter, I wanted to distance humanism from earlier secularists' belief in the inevitability of human progress. It was why, when discussing Primo Levi and the Nazi concentration camps, I talked of a *provisional* humanism. I have, in subsequent chapters, defended the idea of there being something special about being human, and on that I have built a defence of the ideal of a fully human life, and the obligation to respect the humanity of others. All too often, however, we humans fail to live a fully human life, and we fail to respect the humanity of others. My humanism is located in that gap between the possible and the actual. It faces the fact of the drab and complacent lives which people lead when they fail to use to the full their powers of intellect and imagination and feeling. It acknowledges the terrible record of man's inhumanity to man. These are grounds for sober realism, but not for despair. The ideal to which we can aspire is not a remote non-human ideal. It is one which is formed from our experience of what human beings are capable of at their best. It is an ideal that comes from within our own humanity.

I turn finally to the emphasis on *particularity*. In my discussion of the role of the narrative arts in giving meaning to our lives I suggested that they are able to do this because they present us with particular individuals. I called this a 'paradigmatic particularity' because the individuals who are presented to us in creative literature and the other arts are individuals with whom we can identify, we can recognise their situations and experiences as like our own, but we can identify with them only because they come alive as unique individuals. This combination of particular individuals with shared situations and experiences is also a general feature of the humanism which I want to espouse. It does not deal in abstractions. It is not a 'religion of humanity' in the abstract. I have defended the idea of a shared human nature, giving rise to shared ideals and shared values, but that shared nature, those shared ideals and values, are exhibited by unique individuals in all their endless variety.

Again it is creative literature and other imaginative fictions that do justice to this particularity. I have said that the literature and drama of tragedy are reminders of human fragility and failure. The fact of the unique and irreducible particularity of individuals is captured by the literature and drama of comedy.[10] A writer such as Dickens is a great humanist (as well as a rather woolly Christian) because he creates a wealth of absurd and flawed individuals all of whom we can recognise and in all of whom we can see something of ourselves. I have said that to understand the importance of tragedy does not mean that life is irredeemably tragic. Likewise to look at human beings from the perspective of comedy is not to say that life is just a joke. Still, humour is essential to humanism. It is one of the sources of hope that, for all the experience of grief and loss, of weakness and failure, we can go on laughing at life.[11]

Postscript: Organised Humanism

I have emphasised throughout this book that the views which I defend are my own and should not be regarded as a statement of any humanist doctrine or orthodoxy, for there is none. There is, however, as I stated in the first chapter, an organised secular humanist movement, and my views have been shaped by participation in that movement. This book owes much to discussions which I have enjoyed over recent years with fellow humanists, especially in the British Humanist Association (BHA), the Humanist Philosophers' Group, and East Kent Humanists. The book makes use of some passages from my contributions to the pamphlet *What is Humanism?*, produced by the Humanist Philosophers' Group and published by the British Humanist Association (London, 2002). I am grateful to the BHA for permission to use them.

There are humanist organisations in many countries, and if you would like to know more about them you can obtain information from websites such as the following:

British Humanist Association: www.humanism.org.uk
American Humanist Association: www.americanhumanist.org
International Humanist and Ethical Union (IHEU): www.iheu.org

The BHA and IHEU share the same postal address: 1 Gower Street, London WC1E 6HD, UK.

Notes

ONE   INTRODUCTION

1 William Shakespeare, *Hamlet*, Act II, scene ii.

2 Giovanni Pico della Mirandola, *On the Dignity of Man and Other Works*, translated by Charles Glen Wallis, with an introduction by Paul J. W. Miller (Indianapolis and New York, 1965), pp. 4–5.

3 Bertrand Russell, *Why I Am Not a Christian and The Faith of a Rationalist* (London, 1983), p. 26.

4 Jean-Paul Sartre, *Existentialism and Humanism*, translated by Philip Mairet (London, 1948), pp. 54–5.

5 Augusto Campana, 'The Origin of the Word "Humanist" ', *Journal of the Warburg and Courtauld Institutes*, vol. IX (1946); Paul Oskar Kristeller, *Renaissance Thought: The Classic, Scholastic and Humanist Strains* (New York, 1961); Kristeller, 'Humanism', in *The Cambridge History of Renaissance Philosophy*, ed. Charles B. Schmitt and Quentin Skinner (Cambridge, 1988). The earliest use of the word 'humaniste' in French is in 1552 (see Campana, p. 70), and the Oxford English Dictionary gives the earliest occurrence of the English word 'humanist', used in this same sense, as 1589. An exhaustive survey of the history of the different uses of the word 'humanism' can be found in Nicholas Walter, *Humanism: What's in the Word* (London, 1997).

6 Jacob Burckhardt, *The Civilization of the Renaissance in Italy* (Oxford, 1981), p. 120. The passage comes in the section 'The Humanists' of Part III 'The Revival of Antiquity'.

7 John Addington Symonds, *The Renaissance in Italy*, vol. II 'The Revival of Learning' (1904 edition, London), p. 52.

8 The English translation is Baron d'Holbach, *The System of Nature*, vol. 1

(Manchester, 1999), introduced by Michael Bush, adapted from the original translation by H. D. Robinson, 1868.

9 Ibid., p. 7.

10 *The Essence of Christianity* was translated into English by the novelist George Eliot. There is a more recent translation of the introduction in *The Fiery Brook: Selected Writings of Ludwig Feuerbach*, translated with an introduction by Zawar Hanfi (New York, 1972).

11 Karl Marx, 'Economic and Philosophic Manuscripts', in *Karl Marx: Selected Writings*, ed. David McLellan (Oxford, 1977), p. 95.

12 Ibid., p. 89.

13 Primo Levi, *If This Is a Man* and *The Truce* (London, 1987), pp. 32–3.

14 Ibid., pp. 46–7.

15 Ibid., pp. 125–8.

16 Ibid., Afterword, p. 398.

TWO   WHY SCIENCE UNDERMINES RELIGION

1 William Paley, *Natural Theology; or, Evidences of the Existence and Attributes of the Deity, Collected from the Appearances of Nature* (London, 1802), ch. III, pp. 19–20.

2 Ibid., ch. V, p. 68.

3 Charles Darwin, *The Origin of Species by Means of Natural Selection or the Preservation of Favoured Races in the Struggle for Life* (Oxford, 1951), ch.15, pp. 536–7.

4 Ibid., p. 537.

5 Ibid., p. 538.

6 Ibid., pp. 538–9.

7 An example of this reformulation of the argument from design is Richard Swinburne, *Is There a God?* (Oxford, 1996). There is a shorter version of his argument in the periodical *Think*, no. 1 (2002), and it is criticised by me and by others in *Think*, no. 4 (2003).

8 A classic text is Jean-François Lyotard, *The Postmodern Condition: A Report on Knowledge* (English trans., Manchester, 1984), especially pp. 31–41.

9 For an amusing critical discussion of creationists' resort to *ad hoc* moves, see Stephen Law's Darwin Day Lecture 'Is Creationism Scientific?' (February 2003) at http://www.humanism.org.uk, and the chapter with the same title in his book *The Philosophy Gym* (London, 2003).

THREE WHAT'S SO SPECIAL ABOUT HUMAN BEINGS?

1 The classic texts are René Descartes, *Discourse on the Method of Properly Conducting One's Reason and of Seeking the Truth in the Sciences* (first published 1637, usually referred to as the 'Discourse on Method'), and *Meditations on the First Philosophy* (first published 1641, usually referred to as the 'Meditations'). There are various English translations of both works readily available.

2 Michel Foucault, *The Order of Things* (London, 1970), pp. 386–7.

3 In trying to understand this material I have been helped by Kate Soper, *Humanism and Anti-Humanism* (London, 1986).

4 Friedrich Nietzsche, *Beyond Good and Evil*, translated by R. J. Hollingdale (Harmondsworth, 1973), section 16.

5 Ibid., section 17.

6 Ibid., section 12.

7 David Hume, *A Treatise of Human Nature*, I.IV.6.

8 Jean-Paul Sartre, *Being and Nothingness*, translated by Hazel Barnes (London, 1957), Part 1, ch. 2, section I.

9 Roland Barthes, *Mythologies* (English trans., St Alban's, 1972), pp. 100–1.

10 *Genesis* (English trans., 1611), book 1, verse 26.

11 John Gray, *Straw Dogs* (London, 2002), pp. 3–4.

12 Ibid., pp. 5–6.

13 Ibid., pp. 28–9.

FOUR MORALITY IN A GODLESS WORLD

1 See, respectively, *Leviticus* 18.22, 18.19 and 19.26–7. For other amusing examples see Simon Blackburn, *Being Good* (Oxford, 2001), p. 11.

2 The argument goes back to Plato's dialogue *Euthyphro*, at 10a, and is repeated in just about every modern philosophical discussion of the relation between morality and divine commands.

3 David Hume, *A Treatise of Human Nature* (1740), book III, part III, section I, 'Of the Origin of the Natural Virtues and Vices', and *An Enquiry Concerning the Principles of Morals* (1751), section V, 'Why Utility Pleases'.

4 Aristotle, *The Politics*, book I, 1253a 8–19.

5 For example, John McDowell, 'Values and Secondary Qualities', in *Morality and Objectivity*, ed. Ted Honderich (London, 1985). The comparison is criticised in Simon Blackburn, 'Errors and the Phenomenology of Value', in the same volume.

6 John Stuart Mill, *Utilitarianism* (1861; many subsequent editions), ch. II.

7 The demanding character of utilitarian morality is very clearly and consistently demonstrated in the work of the philosopher Peter Singer. See, for instance, his book *Practical Ethics* (Oxford, 1979), and his article 'Famine, Affluence and Morality', reprinted in various anthologies including *International Ethics*, edited by Charles R. Beitz, Marshall Cohen, Thomas Scanlon and John A. Simmons (Princeton, 1985), and *Ethics in Practice*, edited by Hugh LaFollette (Oxford, 1997 and 2002).

8 Immanuel Kant, *Groundwork of the Metaphysics of Morals* (1785; many subsequent editions), section 2.

9 Ronald Dworkin, in his *Taking Rights Seriously* (London, 1977), calls this the idea of rights as 'trumps'.

10 See Bernard Williams, *Ethics and the Limits of Philosophy* (London, 1985), ch. 10, 'Morality, the Peculiar Institution'.

11 The classic passage is in Aristotle's *Ethics*, book I, ch. 7, at 1097b 25.

12 Mill, *Utilitarianism*, ch. II.

13 It is a matter for debate whether Mill is consistent in attempting to combine this distinction between higher and lower pleasures with a utilitarianism which stresses that 'the greatest happiness', understood as quantity of pleasure, is the sole test of value. I cannot enter into that debate here. I can only say that, if he is inconsistent, so much the worse for his utilitarianism.

14 These implications of utilitarianism have been vigorously elaborated by Peter Singer; see especially his *Animal Liberation* (London, 1975) and his *Practical Ethics* (Cambridge, 1979).

15 Richard Dawkins, *The Selfish Gene* (Oxford, 1976).

16 An open letter from the bishops of Bradford, Carlisle, Chester, Exeter, Liverpool, Rochester, Southwell and Winchester concerning the appointment of the Bishop of Reading, dated 16 June. In *Guardian*, 19 June 2003.

17 Pope John Paul II, *Evangelium Vitae* (Encyclical Letter, published by the Catholic Truth Society, London, 1995), p. 119.

18 Ibid., p. 132.

FIVE   THE MEANING OF LIFE AND THE NEED FOR STORIES

1 William Shakespeare, *Hamlet*, Act I, scene v.

2 Cf. Richard Dawkins, *Unweaving the Rainbow* (Harmondsworth, 1998).

3 Aristotle, *Metaphysics*, book I, ch. 1, 980a 22.

4 For an excellent discussion of the importance of narratives and the need for stories, see Richard Kearney, *On Stories* (London, 2002 – published in the same series as this book).

5 Virginia Woolf, *To the Lighthouse* (first published 1927; Penguin annotated edition, with introduction and notes by Hermione Lee, Harmondsworth, 1992), introduction, p. xiv. Subsequent references are to page numbers in this edition.

6 Graham Swift, *Waterland* (Picador edition, London, 1984).

7 The text of the Richard Dimbleby lecture, delivered by the Archbishop of Canterbury, Rowan Williams, on 19 December 2002, is at: http://www.guardian.co.uk/Print/0,3858,4571168,00.html

8 The phrase 'The Sea of Faith' was the title of a BBC television series made by the theologian Don Cupitt, which gave rise to the Sea of Faith Network and a magazine with the same title. Some of the people in the network would describe themselves as Christian humanists and their views have much in common with the humanism I present in this book.

9 John Cottingham, in his book *On the Meaning of Life* (London, 2003) – a book in the same series as this one – has some fine things to say about human fragility and vulnerability (pp. 67–73), and he introduces the idea of spirituality as a matter of practices which enable us to come to terms with this vulnerability (p. 79). He then suggests that such practices may lead us to 'intimations of a transcendent world of meaning' (p. 100), and he appears to conclude that, without the hope engendered by these intimations, the 'fragility of our human condition' is liable to leave our lives devoid of meaning (e.g. pp. 69–70, 85, 104). It is this slippage, from the acceptance of fragility to the demand for a transcendent source of consolation, that I want to resist.

10 The monotheistic religions are pretty short on humour. I may be wrong but I don't think there's a single joke in the whole of the Christian Bible. Again the contrast with ancient Greek polytheism is interesting. Book I of Homer's *Iliad*, for instance, ends with the gods having a party: Hephaestus serves the drinks, 'and a fit of helpless laughter seized the happy gods as they watched him bustling up and down the hall' (Book I, lines 599–600, in E. V. Rieu's translation).

11 There is a wonderful recording of the song 'Laughing at Life' by Billie Holiday which is, for me, one of the great expressions of humanism.

Most of her songs are about unrequited love or the pain of parting, and her own emotional life had more than its share of unhappy and destructive relationships. She was at the sharp end of racism, and she was an alcoholic and a drug addict. But her songs, including 'Laughing at Life', express a defiance that makes them a testament to the resilience of the human spirit.

Index